Golf from the
Ground Up

Golf from the Ground Up

BOB MULLEN

Illustrations by
Tom Weyl

Burford Books

Printed in the United States of America.

10   9   8   7   6   5   4   3   2   1

Library of Congress Cataloging-in-Publication Data
Mullen, Bob, 1943–
    Golf from the ground up / Bob Mullen.
            p.   cm.
    Includes bibliographical references.
    ISBN 978-1-58080-154-6
    1. Swing (Golf)—Handbooks, manuals, etc.   2. Golf—Handbooks, manuals, etc.   I. Title.

    GV979.S9M85 2009
    796.352'3—dc22
                                                    2009009358

Contents

Acknowledgments

Learning to teach is a lifelong process, and I am not sure that all of it can be learned. Like any skill, a lot of it comes with the genes. Some of us were just given better tools in certain areas of life, and I am happy I found where my tools worked best before my working days were over. I am very thankful for that.

I cannot possibly thank each and every student who has imparted some bit of golf wisdom for me to absorb, thresh, tumble and blend with other assorted images and thoughts into what has become the methodology you will find in this book, but if you have talked golf with me you will no doubt find some part of something we talked about in here, because I was listening.

I owe a great deal of thanks to my Uncle Dick who taught me the Vardon grip at the age of eleven and allowed me to raid the spare clubs stored on the porch at Grandpa's house. From the group called the "Backsiders" I learned that good golf can be played while having fun. I am grateful for my business partner Scott Henson, without whose help I would not have had the opportunity to study the golf swing with state-of-the-art equipment in an indoor facility. Early in the study of the out-to-in swing I bounced ideas off PGA professional Bobby Stevenson and I owe him a thank you.

Throughout this process I have had excellent support from the USGTF staff and community. "Keep focused on the fundamentals" was Geoff Bryant's advice, and though I come at the teaching from a different perspective, his advice was solid gold.

Thanks to Marilyn, my wife, who is my strongest critic, partner and advocate, to my daughter-in-law Laura Peticolas who took on the physics challenge sorting out and verifying my thoughts on center of mass and writing Laura's law, and to another member of my family Tom Weyl who was actually my college room mate. Tom did all the illustrations in this book. Maybe our book will end up in the Macalester College Library, a place the two of us seldom were during our days at Mac.

A special thanks to my publisher, Peter Burford. From the first day we talked he has supported this book and my ideas with insights of his own. "You have a new approach to teaching golf," he said, "but you need to tell me more." I was anxious to tell him more, all the time fearing at any moment I would hear a dial tone. I didn't, and his faith and patience in what I had to say has resulted in this book. I think you will find what Peter found, just good sound fundamentals starting "from the ground up."

May, 2009
Steamboat Springs, CO

Foreword

As president of The United States Golf Teachers Federation, I was pleased when Bob Mullen asked me to write a foreword for his book, *Golf from the Ground Up*. Bob is a long-time member of the United States Golf Teachers Federation and one of 300 Master Golf Teaching Professionals®. As a result, his insights reflect many time-tested and proven theories. The USGTF encourages its 13,000 teachers to look for new and innovative ways to solve problems in delivering the teaching message to the student. In this book Bob has done just that. The basic golf fundamentals have not changed over time, and Bob did not want to write a book unless he had something new and innovative to say to the golfer. You will only have to read Chapter One to realize that Bob has reached his goal. This is not just another instruction book. Unsatisfied with the ability of his students to retain information and learn skills, Bob went looking for answers, and he found them by researching the discoveries made during the United States and Great Britain's almost simultaneous studies, known today as the "Decades of the Brain." His book begins by providing insights into how adult golfers' brains work, and how their motor skills develop. Bob explains why the brain is boss in motor-skill learning, and why there are no shortcuts to that process. Adult learners will be pleased to find out that the brain remains elastic throughout life, and that learning can and does occur at any age.

The book pioneers a new teaching approach in addressing the fundamentals of golf. Bob calls his approach the "Platform." He has not strayed from teaching the neutral grip, the fundamentals of stance, alignment, and ball position, but he has also added sections on footwork and rotation. Bob believes that these six fundamentals are often neglected in the teaching and learning of the golf swing because we all want to just "hit the ball." It is an interesting concept and is proving successful for his students. He teaches the Platform to his students before he teaches the swing, because he insists that you can't make a good, repeatable swing without a sound Platform.

This is also the first book I've come across to seriously address the major cause of the slice, the out-to-in swing path. No simple answers like swinging over the top, or casting the club. Bob has filmed golfers, studied them on a simulator and admits that at one time he was a victim himself of the number one fault causing the out-to-in swing. It is the push-off. Self-taught golfers employ the push-off to gain additional power in their swings, believing that the golf swing is a power move rather than a speed move. Once the golfer stops moving laterally and begins to understand rotation and weight transfer, the swing can find the correct path. Bob has identified the second most common cause as lazy footwork, and uses Laura's Law to demonstrate how a late transfer of weight to the front foot leads to an out-to-in swing path on lower-handicap golfers. There are other causes as well: not understanding the double pendulum, and misalignment, but Bob finds that 75 percent of the problems begin with the footwork.

Bob's writing style is easy to follow and the drawings give an excellent perspective on each motor skill or drill. In the Author's Notes there are a number of discoveries in store for the reader. Bob will tell you what secret Hogan left out of his book, *Five Lessons*. He will explain why Stupid can ruin a good round of golf and how to keep him out of your bag, and much more.

Whether you are picking up a club for the first time or have been at the game for years, this book will get you started on the right track, or help you refine your thinking. Improvement in the game of golf is a daily task, and we never get too good to quit learning. From the beginner to the professional, most golfers remain students of the game all their lives.

This book should be a welcome addition to your golf library and a valuable asset as you continue playing and learning the game.

GEOFF BRYANT, PRESIDENT
UNITED STATES GOLF TEACHERS FEDERATION

Introduction

"Competitive golf is played mainly on a five-and-a-half-inch course, the space between your ears."

—Bobby Jones

There is only one word I would omit in Mr. Jones' statement: *competitive.* I believe all golf is played on that very same five-and-a-half-inch course. Whether it's for the Master's Championship or for fun on a lighted, par-three course at 11:30 P.M., it's how you, the individual, understand and manage that "course" that determines the outcome of your golfing experience. I love the game of golf, and I love to teach the game of golf. What I want most for my students is that they learn to play with confidence and more than that, I want them to enjoy playing the game as much as I do.

There are over 6,000 books in print on the subject of golf today. To take on the task of writing a new one the author should either be important (which I am not) or have something to say, which I believe I do. It is not only important to have something important to say, it is equally important to express the message so that the readers can understand it. It is nearly impossible to write in such a way that you cannot be misunderstood. The same barriers to learning exist for each person reading this book that exist for each student who takes a lesson on the practice range. I have made extensive use of drawings to clarify every explanation, and I will explain the learning barriers in Chapter One.

Although this book is an instruction book for golfers of all ages, it is directed toward those golfers past the age of twenty. I've written it because so many adults have given up on learning golf or progressing in learning new golf skills. They blame it on tired muscles, creaking bones, or a sore back, or they believe their motor skills have become fixed and have the idea they can't learn or improve. I want you to know that adult motor skills are not fixed. New skills can be learned. If you have been struggling, I want you to know it's not that you can't learn, it's that you haven't been shown the proper learning process. Consequently, you have probably set your expectations too high. Ease back on the throttle just a bit, and you'll find the success you have been looking for; it's not that far away.

I grew up in the day when inkwell desks made of hardwood, supported by wrought iron legs bolted to the floor, were still in the classrooms. I went to the same grade school as my dad and his brothers, and I even had the same second grade teacher. Teachers were respected in those days, and it takes hard work and dedication to become a teacher like the ones I remember. They not only taught, but they also inspired us to learn. To them teaching was more of a calling than an occupation. I am a teacher, and I like the title. I aspire to be as good as the ones I remember. To achieve a breakthrough in understanding with a student takes time, and those *Ah ha* moments are priceless. Every good teacher I know goes on learning every day they teach. Each student I work with brings a lesson to me, and you can't imagine what a wealth of knowledge that creates.

I wasn't always a teacher. I received a first-rate education at one of the finest colleges in the country, I excelled in sports (lettered nine times in college), I was a combat Marine in Vietnam (decorated twice for bravery), I was a manufacturing supervisor, I've been to the Business School at

Harvard, I was a businessman (we successfully took our company public), but when it's all said and done the thing I am happiest about is being a teacher. Nothing compares to sharing knowledge. I was never a pro golfer. I hit my first golf balls in Maple Grove Cemetery to a closely mowed area between some tightly spaced head stones over 50 years ago. I have played and loved the game of golf ever since.

I am a USGTF Master Teacher, one of fewer than 300 in the country. I started the Steamboat Short-Game School thirteen years ago, and in 2005 we opened All Seasons Golf, an indoor teaching facility where I could teach year-round here in Northwest Colorado. As a teacher of both golf and skiing, I've had adult students come to me and say they just weren't learning like they used to. They were frustrated, and that frustrated me. I felt I was failing them as a teacher. Like any teacher with a problem, I went looking for answers. The fundamentals were sound, but the students did not retain them. The question was, why? I found the answer wasn't in what I was teaching, but how I was teaching. In the 1990s, the United States and Great Britain both established what they called the Decade of the Brain. Both countries spent huge sums of money bringing together the top psychologists, neurologists, and other individuals connected with the study of the brain to share their knowledge and discoveries. The purpose was to further the overall advancement of brain science.

Thanks to that combined twenty years of collaboration and a wealth of new research in learning and retention of motor skills, we now know that the methods we used in the past are not effective in teaching motor skills to adult students. The discoveries continue, but what we know now is that adults need to understand what they are learning, and how they learn. In addition, they need prompt and informative feedback, and most of all they need time to absorb the motor skill. We cannot rush the process. The learning methods and the explanations in my book are based on my understanding and knowledge of the most recent studies in neurology and psychology. I explain how your brain works when you are learning a golf skill, and how you can establish a realistic set of expectations.

I have changed my approach to teaching, and it has made a world of difference to my students. They are under less pressure to reach for unrealistic goals, and by understanding how the brain learns motor skills, we can improve the teaching and learning process. I explain the brain's use of the transfer process so you are aware of it during your self-teaching. I explain how each fundamental works and how and why it is important to the swing. I believe you will find it will give you new knowledge and confidence as you pursue golf in the future.

Over our lifetimes we have mastered some very complicated motor skills. Most of these movements we mastered before we were able to speak. We can all be thankful for that. Can you imagine how difficult it would have been to learn to walk if our mothers had to explain the movements to us? Some of us would still be on the floor. So, how does this relate to golf?

We already have a great number of the basic skills: standing, rotation, swinging our arms, gripping, distance perception, and others. If we start with the skills we already own and build from these, we have a very good chance of developing a sound golf game with solid fundamentals. This assumes a couple of things. The first is that you read the first chapter and commit to what you will learn about your brain and how it works. Second, you will commit to the drills and the time involved developing the motor skills as they apply to golf fundamentals. Practice it, use it, or lose it, is a fact.

During this process we will not learn the golf swing first. The swing will be the easiest part of learning the game of golf, because it is the most fun. (You get to hit balls, you get to see results, and you get real feedback.) Instead we are first going to focus on a set of fundamentals that support the golf swing. Individually these skills are boring to work on and for that reason often are neglected, but they are highly critical parts of your golf game. I call this part of your game the **Platform**.

The golfer needs to know all the elements of the platform before he/she can perform the golf swing properly.

I want you to think of the platform—the synergy of the grip, stance, footwork, rotation, alignment, and ball position—as a single entity, and as important as the swing. You can't learn or perform a repeatable swing until you master the fundamentals of the platform. In the future you will look at an errant shot and think about what errors might have been made in the platform that would have contributed to that type of mistake. Faults in the platform lead to bad swings. Get your platform fundamentals correct and the swing corrects itself. When swing faults are repaired with quick fixes by altering the fundamentals of the platform, they lead to additional faults. I call these quick fixes bandaids. The simple fact is you can't fix faults with faults, and quick fixes seldom follow the fundamentals.

The first and most important fundamental skill is the grip. If you don't have a grip, you will never have a game. The next skills we will learn are directed toward keeping you in balance while allowing you to swing. They are your stance, footwork, and rotation. Have you ever thought about your balance in relation to golf? Since you are not running or jumping or moving much, how significant could balance be? I consider it the most critical ability in any athletic movement. A proper stance combined with proper footwork allows the golfer to rotate while maintaining balance so a repeatable swing can happen. Your brain receives input from your eyes, the semi-circular canals in your inner ear, pressure receptors in your skin (especially the feet and hands), and stretch receptors in your muscles and joints. All this information needs to be put to use to build your golf swing, and the platform is the place where the majority of this happens.

Do you understand conversion and diversion (two terms critical to alignment)? How do you rotate your shoulders and hips? Where is the ball placed when you take your stance? What is the first move in the takeaway? Did you know there are two pendulums in your golf swing? It all starts *from the ground up*. Solid fundamentals starting with the platform assure that you can make a repeatable swing.

Let me emphasize we are all looking for a repeatable swing, not a perfect swing. We want a swing that produces predictable results. If you know where your ball is going, you can manage your golf game. You can score, and that is the point of the game of golf. You do not have to swing like a tour player to accomplish this. The tour player's swing has been developed over years of practice, usually from a very young age. It is the result of hitting thousands and thousands of balls. The perfection of the tour swing has nothing to do with you or your swing. I have a number of students report great success and lower scores after correcting their grip and stabilizing their platforms. The consistency of their swings improved dramatically.

The average self-taught amateur gets his swing from *transfer*, combining a number of previously learned swinging skills into a *golf swing*. This swing can be entirely functional and repeatable when attached to the platform. The trouble for the amateur usually begins when he or she takes a lesson, and the instructor only knows one swing to teach. "Here, swing like me." Or, the amateur looks at swing photos in a magazine and tries to swing like the pictures. I believe that both of these examples can be recipes for disaster.

You may never swing like a pro, and in attempting to do so you may ruin a perfectly good golf swing. What you do have the time to understand and learn are the fundamentals that will make *your* swing work time after time. The most important thing is to learn to be a swinger and not a hitter. Hitters have all kinds of problems, and most of them start with the hands and an out-to-in swing path. The secret of the swing is not really a secret. We all seem to know how to swing the golf club when we make a practice swing. The secret is how to use that *swing* when we hit a ball.

Once again, it's in the fundamentals. Knowledge of the platform fundamentals will prepare you to make this happen. You have to let those fundamentals work for you when you play. I will explain how the backswing and downswing work, and how the physics of the double pendulum allows you to develop tremendous speed with little effort coming on a path from in-to-out-to-in. You will learn to let your arms and hands play a more passive role and become a swinger and not a hitter. It is a proper swing technique—not strength—that delivers the 300-yard drive.

And, remember, no one ever said that you had to swing pretty to shoot par. Swing in-to-out-to-in, extend toward the target, and make your swing repeatable.

The out-to-in swing path is a problem that affects 90 percent of all golfers. It causes the common slice and for some, the pull-hook. If you are like most golfers you stand on the tee box, aim somewhere left of center, and watch your ball travel from left to right, time and again, hoping you allowed enough *windage* to keep the ball in play. I expect you have searched for the cure, listened to friends (who probably were fighting the same problem), taken lessons when you could afford them, and each time you got the same advice: "You are swinging over the top."

I'm sure you are tired of trying solutions that haven't worked and listening to explanations that didn't seem to fit your particular swing problem. You might be thinking you are stuck with your out-to-in swing path. My first answer to those who want to correct this problem is, "Remember in golf there are no quick fixes. The cure will be in the fundamentals." We can fix that problem once you understand what you are doing and why you do it. There are a number of causes for the out-to-in swing problem. You may have just one, or you may have a combination of problems. Curing this fault will take hard work. You didn't get stuck on the out-to-in path overnight, and it will not move in-to-out-to-in overnight.

Every month there's a new article in your favorite golf magazine promising a quick cure to every golf problem known to man; every day there's a gizmo advertised on golf TV; you could buy something every week that promises to be the shortcut to overnight success. These devices are worn in various ways, hit through, swung, wrapped around the body, stood on, looked through, poked into the ground, and who knows what else, all promising that the device or the cure will replace hard work and practice. Truth is, it won't. Somehow, out of all this information, some good, some bad, the average golfer is supposed to get a picture of how to become a better golfer. No one ever said it better than Harvey Penick:

"Golf tips are like aspirin. One may do you good, but if you swallow the whole bottle you will be lucky to survive."

As a teacher, I am embarassed by the snake oil aspect of the barrage of ideas in many of the articles and the game-improvement products thrust on the golfing public. They sell magazines, and put money in somebody's pocket, but I doubt that they really help the golfer. The game of golf is hard enough to master without sending students down side roads with promised quick fixes, and handing them aids that only delay their understanding and mastery of the fundamentals.

Those of us who have played golf our whole lives know the game remains a puzzle, an enigma, an ever-changing dream, chased by all who step to the first tee. Somewhere in the mind of us all lingers the hope, "Will this be the day I finally get it all together?" The journey to learn the game of golf is never-ending. We cannot master golf. For every triumph there will be a failure, good shots will be followed by bad, and just when we think things can't get worse, they will. Those of us who teach know that the more we teach and the more we play, the more we learn, and the process never stops. Most teachers would agree with me that if we could find some of our first students, we would like to give them their money back. I learn my golf from reading, playing, experimenting, taking lessons, giving lessons, throwing out what doesn't work and repeating the process. My love for the game, oddly enough, began in the cemetery behind my boyhood home, and I suspect it will end in a similar place.

In putting together what I have to say I have made every effort to stick as closely as possible to the basic fundamentals of the game of golf. The new information I have added is about how our brain learns motor skills after the age of twenty, and how we can use that information to establish realistic goals to learn or improve our game. I have introduced the platform (grip, alignment, stance, ball position plus footwork and rotation) in the strong hope that more emphasis will be placed on fundamentals supporting the swing, and the importance of learning the platform first. I have explained the difference between a golf *swing* and a *hit,* and how the swing works with your platform. The hardest swing problem to fix in golf is the out-to-in swing path. The reason for this is the number of causes. Some are obvious and some are hidden. I believe I have explained them all, and how you can use the fundamentals to correct the problems.

I hope that this book turns out to be as good a teacher for you as the many books I have read and the many teachers and students I have worked with have been for me.

1

The Brain Is Boss

"If the brain were simple enough for us to understand it, we would be too simple to understand it."

—KEN HILL

Since my days as a young athlete I can remember coaches talking about muscle memory, and how important it was to practice movements over and over until you trained the muscles to remember the movements. Once you had the muscle memory, you could rely on the muscles to repeat the activity automatically. When you failed at something, it was clear that you just hadn't practiced hard enough or long enough to create the proper muscle memory.

Today I still hear some teaching professionals talking about muscle memory, and it surprises me. Most of you probably remember in biology we hooked up some detached frog legs to a battery, and we could stimulate movement by sending an electrical charge to the muscles. In my day the boys loved it, or at least had to pretend they did, and the girls had to act squeamish. My daughters would tell me times have changed since then,

THE BOSS

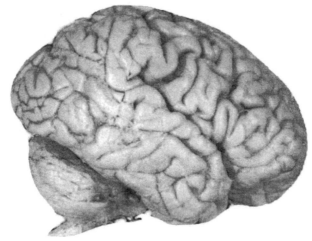

and my granddaughter, who at age ten just dissected a chicken, would just laugh. Needless to say, it has long been common knowledge that muscles have no memory; they are stimulated to movement by electrical impulses that arrive along the central nervous system from signals that originate in the brain. It is clear that the brain is the Boss. When we learn motor skills, we are teaching the brain, not the muscles. When we teach the brain we must overcome a number of barriers, and overcoming them allows us to learn new skills. Some of these barriers are imposed by the physiology of the brain, others are imposed by us (psychological), and there are still other barriers imposed by time and our willingness to exert the effort.

Let's talk about the **physiological** barrier. The human brain is truly amazing. The more I learn, the more I realize how important it is to teach within the context of the brain's evolving plan. After about the age of twenty our brains make a change. Up until that time, the brain needed to accept input on motor skills at a rapid pace. The purpose was of course to protect the organism. The brain seems to know we needed to run, to fight, to build, to clothe ourselves, to protect ourselves, to feed ourselves. In short, we needed to survive; our brain was primed to collect motor skills that would make sure this would happen. All you have to do is watch young children play games to realize that they are on a different level than adults when it comes to learning motor skills. After age twenty the brain reaches a certain maturity level. It now becomes protective of the skills it has learned, and it does not accept new motor skills as readily as it did in our youth.

In our youth our brain was willing to move quickly through the three stages of motor skill learning:

1. The *cognitive stage,* where the neurons gather information from the senses. Think of this stage as the one where you gather information from all your books, notes, graphs, maps, pictures, and whatever else you might need in preparation to take a test.

2. The *associative stage* is the building stage where practice and visualization strengthen the bundle of neurons; the release of brain chemicals is important during this process. Think of this stage as study time. In this stage you are doing the skill. The more often you do the skill and the more varied ways you do it, the more effective your use of time will be, and the stronger you will build the bundle of neurons that controls the motor skill.

3. The *autonomous stage* is when the bundle of neurons is controlled by the cerebellum. At this stage the motor skill has been learned and can be carried out without thinking. This does not mean that you have the perfect swing because years of fine tuning lies ahead to perfect the movement, but you no longer have to think about the motions.

The neurologists tell us that after age twenty, the brain changes and would rather substitute known skills, those already in the autonomous stage, than go through the process of developing new ones (creating new neuron bundles). This substitution is known as transfer. There are still millions and millions of unused neurons available and plenty of unused space, but the brain now becomes frugal in its selection of new motor skills.

So what are you to do? Well, its not your fault that your brain now wants to substitute previously learned skills for new ones, you just have to be aware that it is going to do this and make that knowledge work for you. This can work out okay if the substituted skills match–this transfer can speed the learning process. However, transfer leads to problems when the old skill and the new skill don't match. The process can be really harmful if you don't recognize what is happening and understand why you are blocked, and why the new skill seems impossible to learn. This happens a lot in the game of golf. The causes for blocking are:

> ➤ Self-teaching without complete understanding of the new motor skill involved, or the time required for learning the skill.
> ➤ Lessons without follow-up, insufficient practice time, or incorrect practice of the skills presented.
> ➤ Golfers who are constantly looking for quick cures or fixes and, for that reason, never spend enough time on any one thing to learn it.

In each situation the motor skill does not go beyond the cognitive stage, before it is replaced by a different skill the golfer is attempting to learn or an old skill the golfer already has in the autonomous stage. The learning period for motor skills for the average adult is three to four weeks. Few students put in sufficient effort to master any skill before they move on to something new. Learning the game or changing your game is hard work, but well worth the time spent. Golf is a hard game to learn, so don't let it discourage you. Golf will test your determination to learn.

The second barrier to learning is **psychological**. This is probably the most important factor, because you can't learn if you don't believe you can learn, or if you don't believe fully in what you are learning. You can't learn if you give up the first time your new skill fails (the old, "I knew that wouldn't work," or "I tried that before" attitude). You have to believe in yourself, and you have to believe in the change. In order to learn any new skill you have to tell your brain the new skill is important to your success. Since this process will take three to four weeks it will be a battle—your brain doesn't need the new skill; it was happy the way it was. Your lack of success may convince you that you can't change ("I can't learn"), and your errant shots may eat away at your confidence and determination. "What was so bad about my old swing?" Or "golf is just too hard." Just remember that if you quit, you will have another partially learned skill in your frontal cortex, cluttering things up.

I know some of you are reading this and thinking that three to four weeks is probably necessary for someone else, but not for me. I can learn anything in a week or even less. Well, I congratulate you on your optimism, but let me remind you that the greatest golfer we have ever seen, Tiger Woods, took *one full year* to make his swing change, so plan on at "least" three weeks per motor skill. If you do it faster, congratulations! But, I suspect that in your hurry to master something like the grip in just a couple of days, you will end up down the road with the combination weed whacker-pooper-scooper grip used by the infamous Dub Chunks, known mostly for never owning an old golf ball. Who's the boss? You? No, it's your brain.

"Don't Overbook the Cerebral Cortex"

The maximum number of new motor skills that can be accommodated in the cerebral cortex at one time is one. The motor skill will be under the control of the cerebral cortex for a period lasting up to four weeks, while it goes through the cognitive and associative stages before becoming a motor skill that you can build upon. It is made stronger by chemical exchange along the synapses occurring between the neurons. If this work is interrupted by the introduction of another motor skill, the cerebral cortex will cease work on the first motor skill and move to the new motor skill. This is one of the discoveries of the Decade of the Brain, and probably explains why so much is lost when lessons are given on a weekly basis and new skills are introduced too rapidly.

In the weekly lesson scenario, the student is eager to move forward, and the instructor is eager to see progress. A student with good cognitive skills and coordination will be able to perform at a reasonably high level on the prior week's motor skill task, even though the motor skill has not been fully learned. This gives both the student and the instructor the impression that the skill has been mastered. This is where too little knowledge about how the brain works will get both the student and the instructor in trouble. The student will now be given new motor skill tasks, and the student's brain will begin to put its cognitive skills to work on these tasks. Remember: The brain cannot work on learning two motor skills at one time. The student and instructor have taken the progress of the prior week away from the student by loading his or her brain with a new motor skill. The cognitive brain has a new task and is now going to work on it. The brain will substitute an alternate skill for the one that was in progress. This is how the game of golf gets partially learned, and at the end of your series of lessons, you wonder once again why your game doesn't improve.

Brain chemicals make up another important factor in the process of building motor skills. The neurons are the storage medium, and they are fed information by dendrites and connected by synapses. The stronger the neuron bundle, the stronger the motor skill. The synapses are the connections between the neurons, and they grow stronger when we practice. Another key to synaptic growth is emotion; the more emotion we feel, the more chemicals we produce. This leads to stronger synaptic connections. Motor skill learning is facilitated by emotional investment. Competitive learning sessions create emotion. We also should be celebrating positive performance. In an effort to remain cool we hardly react to our really terrific shots and putts. This does not build stronger neuron bundles.

As individuals, we usually react more strongly to bad tee shots and missed short putts. This gives a stronger chemical reinforcement to our poorest shots and makes it more likely that we will repeat them. When something goes wrong, resist the urge to react. Remain neutral; the shot is over. Put your energy into reinforcing the neurons that produce the good shots.

If we want positive results we must process information from start to finish, provide ample practice time and strong accurate feedback, and celebrate good performance. The neurons (and it takes millions) will in due time grow a strong enough bond so that the cerebellum can cause these motor skills to be performed automatically. This is where sequences of skills can be routed with higher rates of speed, much greater accuracy, and less effort. This is the autonomous stage and the next step in improved performance. You will spend years of practice refining and tuning, trying for perfection. Sorry to say that in our game perfection seldom comes, and when it does it is only a visitor. But, there is no reason you can't enjoy the quest for a more perfect game.

In summary I want to emphasize the following points:

1. Your brain needs time to learn motor skills. The time will vary, but expect it to take as much as four weeks.
2. Your brain needs to be convinced that the skill you are working on is important. Don't give the learning process a half-hearted effort.
3. Your brain can learn only one motor skill at a time. Do not overschedule.
4. Your brain responds to emotion. Be excited about positive results and do not react to poor results.
5. Use it or lose it. Continued practice is necessary to keep the motor skill finely tuned.

2

The
Platform

"Any method, old or new, will fail if, first, it is not founded on sound fundamentals and, second, if the golfer trying to master it will not force or train or cajole himself into mastering those fundamentals before he attends to the frills."

—JACK NICKLAUS

In the introduction I explained the importance of the platform. This is without a doubt the boring side of golf. No booming drives, no balls bouncing close to the pin, no putts making that familiar sound as they find the bottom of the cup. Boring? You bet! Necessary? Absolutely! This is where every great game of golf found its beginning. It's where the smallest of mistakes can lead to major problems, and yet it is the most neglected part of every amateur's golf game.

PGA teachers base their teaching of the setup on the concept of GASP (grip, alignment, stance and ball position). These fundamentals are taught in every golf school by nearly every instructor you'll meet. I simply don't believe the concept of GASP goes far enough or is emphasized enough

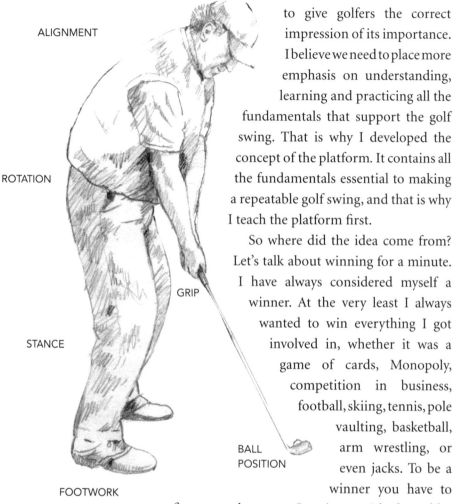

ALIGNMENT

ROTATION

GRIP

STANCE

BALL
POSITION

FOOTWORK

to give golfers the correct impression of its importance. I believe we need to place more emphasis on understanding, learning and practicing all the fundamentals that support the golf swing. That is why I developed the concept of the platform. It contains all the fundamentals essential to making a repeatable golf swing, and that is why I teach the platform first.

So where did the idea come from? Let's talk about winning for a minute. I have always considered myself a winner. At the very least I always wanted to win everything I got involved in, whether it was a game of cards, Monopoly, competition in business, football, skiing, tennis, pole vaulting, basketball, arm wrestling, or even jacks. To be a winner you have to figure out the game. Growing up, I had an older brother and most of the neighborhood games involved older boys. My brother and his friends were not about to lose to someone younger, so the competition was always fierce. I received little coaching, and I had to play well enough to get included. I got pretty good at figuring out most games except one, and that game didn't involve my older brother.

I hate to admit this, but it involved girls, and it was the one game I never won: jacks. I watched how they did it, but I could never win. As they sat on the sidewalks the girls moved easily through the ones and twos and threes and so on, with right leg tucked under and left leg stretched out, skirt folded to make a basket for the jacks, all so organized and all done the same way every time. I took their challenges, but I never won. I rationalized that it was because I never practiced, but it was way more than that.

I know now that I never sat the same way and experimented every time I played, but none of the girls did. They just sat there with right leg folded in, and their left leg extended, and cleaned my clock every time. You have no idea how much losing to the girls hurt. It was my first introduction to the concept of a platform, but I wouldn't know it for about fifty years.

What these young ladies had discovered without the help of any coach was that you need a sound platform to reproduce any athletic movement (motor skill) over and over. In this case, the skill they reproduced was throwing up a ball with one hand, and then with the same hand moving the jacks in a predetermined manner into the other hand, finally catching the ball after one bounce.

In golf we have a different goal, but it requires a platform just the same. We have to hit a ball—oddly it's a golf ball, the same ball the girls used to play jacks—with a golf club, with the intention of ending up in a 4¼ inch hole. The distance to the hole varies, so the manufacturers of the golf clubs have designed clubs of different lengths and heads to produce different trajectories. Because of this we are able use the same swing to produce different distances. We only have to have a repeatable swing, but to have a repeatable swing we need a *platform*.

You might be saying, "I've got a pretty good game right now, and I've never heard of any of this." My answer is the same that I give to everyone: "If you shoot par, I congratulate you, and you, like the jacks girls, have found a sound platform on your own. If you don't shoot par, then the lack of a sound platform is probably the major contributor to your lack of consistent shot-making, and until you develop those six fundamentals you will not get any better, no matter how hard you practice your swing."

It's a lot like building a house. Without pouring a good foundation, sooner or later (and probably sooner) the house begins to shift. That's what will happen with your swing, and no matter how hard you work there are no simple fixes that will put your game back on the right track. Another example is that of a large-tracked vehicle on which sits a crane. From the crane hangs a cable, and attached to the cable is a wrecking ball. It is your job to smash the wrecking ball into a small building in between two larger buildings, and obviously you are not to hit either of the larger buildings. In order to be certain that the direction of the wrecking ball will be accurate you will make a great effort to establish a level and locked location for your tracked vehicle. You will make certain that the tracked vehicle you are going to swing your wrecking ball from is firmly locked in the proper place, so that there will be no chance that you will hit the other buildings. Think of that vehicle as your platform. Why does the platform improve your golf swing? Because the platform does not change.

The elements of the Platform are:

1. **Grip:** The grip section teaches you how to hold the club correctly. Don't start now with the thought, "I like my grip just fine." We won't be getting

along. There are only three correct grips. Period. They are all neutral, which means they do not affect the flight of the ball. If you have a different grip, your grip is affecting the flight of the ball. This defeats the purpose of a stable platform. Choose one of the grip methods and learn it. Once you master the fundamentals of a correct grip, you will begin to feel new unity with your golf club. This will help to develop soft hands around the greens, and increase the accuracy and speed of the all-important hinge that the wrists provide.

2. **Footwork:** Footwork must be learned and practiced. You never get too good to practice your footwork. This is the key to the in-to-out-to-in swing. Very few golfers who have proper footwork swing out-to-in. The drills will keep you from getting lazy in your swing and will keep you extending toward the target, creating accuracy and distance. Good footwork is also the key to good balance.

3. **Rotation:** Rotation is the engine of the golf swing. Proper rotation goes hand in hand with proper footwork. Without proper rotation you cannot make a repeatable golf swing. Rotation can be learned and practiced without a golf club. The drills should be done in front of a mirror so that you can see your hips turn, and your shoulders turn as they follow the hips in the downswing. When you rotate your shoulders you will find that your arms and hands follow this rotation with little or no effort. The rotation moves the club head, not your hands.

4. **Stance:** The proper stance allows you to rotate freely using the large muscles in the center of your body, the shoulders, torso, hips, and the legs, while the arms swing freely. It positions your feet to provide a stable base, providing balance and control of your center of mass. A proper stance improves swing speed and accuracy.

5. **Alignment:** Convergence and divergence: understanding these two words and how they apply to golf will go a long way in helping you line up your shots. This section tells you how to use the bones of your body like the framework of the crane to line up correctly every time. Improper alignment causes many problems for middle and high handicappers. Most of this difficulty comes from not paying attention.

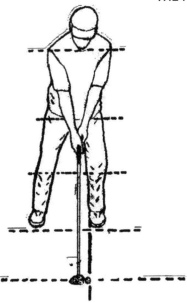

6. **Ball Position:** This is a problem for most amateur golfers. The question of the day is, where do I put the ball? Like everything else in the platform, the ball has a fixed position for every club. In this section you will learn where it goes and why.

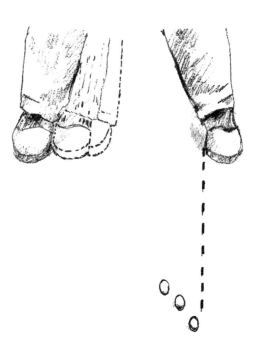

Pre-Shot Routine: I do not call this part of the platform, but it is an important part of learning to play the game of golf successfully. In this section I explain how to prepare to hit a shot. You need a routine and a ritual. There are no reaction shots in golf, so every time you prepare to hit the ball it is as if you were starting over. This fact is what makes golf so difficult. A sound routine prepares you to swing, and a ritual keeps you from over-thinking how you do it.

Okay, you are saying, nice pitch, Bob, but how do I know that all this work you are asking me to do is going to pay off? If I were to tell you, if we lined up all the famous golfers in the world they would all agree most of the mistakes in golf occur before you ever swing the club, would you think that was enough incentive to get started? If you don't, I believe I can round up some of the girls who used to whip me at jacks.

The Grip

"Golf begins with a good grip."
—Ben Hogan

It's Hogan's quote, but Palmer, Snead, Nicklaus, Woods or just about any champion golfer could have said it. How important is our grip when it comes to our success in playing good golf? You will notice that the question is not how important is the grip in our success in hitting the golf ball, but to playing good golf. You can hit the golf ball with just about any grip. There are over twenty million golfers proving that today, but how many of them are successful? Arnold Palmer feels that anyone with a proper grip has something that only one in fifty golfers possessed, and Sam Snead said it was the most common flaw that he saw in the thousands of amateurs he had seen play over his career. The grip connects everything you do to the club. If your grip allows the club's face to be as much as one half of one degree out of square to the target line, the ball can be as much as twenty yards left or right of the target when it finishes. So we can say that if you master the grip, you are doing something that only five out of 100 golfers do correctly.

The grip is the very first thing I look at when someone comes to me for a lesson. If they don't have a sound grip, nothing else I help them with is really going to result in the positive outcome they are looking for.

The bad grip is so prevalent that golf-glove manufacturers have started making golf gloves with a special feature that protects against wear on the heel of your glove. Your golf glove only wears in that particular spot when you have a bad grip. Next time you purchase a golf glove (or maybe you already have one of the new ones), check for the glove with padding on the heel pad. Manufacturers produce clubs to help correct the slice and the hook, and now they are marketing gloves so you don't need to learn to grip the club correctly. These products are being sold in pro shops every day. I would rather teach you how to hold the golf club so you don't need the extra padding.

Now back to the original question. How important is the grip to our success in golf? It is our only contact point with the club. Our hands provide us with touch and feel and control. Our hands also act as a hinge for the second pendulum of the golf swing (more about pendulums later), and allow the club head to line up squarely with the ball-target line. So the answer to the question is: *The grip is all important.* Yet most golfers grab the club and with just a few minutes devoted to grip instruction they begin swinging. Seldom, if ever, do they practice or check their grip. If that is the way you began playing golf, I am asking you to start over. If you are just starting, I am asking you to pay careful attention to the information in this section. Your success as a golfer depends on how well you master the golf grip. This process can take as long as three weeks, and yes, I'm not kidding.

I will describe three different grips that are basically the same. They are all neutral, which means they will not influence the ball flight. We do not want the way we hold the club to make the ball go left or right. We do not want the ball to leave the club with side spin because of our grip. I want you to take a look at the three methods and choose one to make your own. These are the correct ways to grip a golf club. If your grip does not match one of these methods then it is wrong. If you came to me with a problem and said, "I moved my right hand under to compensate for . . ." My answer to you would be, "Let's get your grip corrected, and then let's check out the remainder of your platform." I want you to have a neutral, repeatable platform and that includes a neutral grip. We do that before we assume there is anything wrong with your swing. In that way we will not be sticking a bandaid on the problem.

The learning process for the grip will take a minimum of twenty minutes a day during the learning period. The twenty minutes will be made up of short sessions of five to ten minutes of maximum concentration. Learning the grip (or relearning) is difficult, but you must spend the time. At the end, when you place your hands on the golf club in a darkened room, the positioning will be automatic. Remember, this will take about three weeks. When you self-teach the grip watch for these problems:

1. You began gripping things as a newborn and you have been developing gripping skills since that day. Your brain has already stored lots of grips, but none of them is matched to the gripping of a golf club. If you attempt to grip the club like you grip a baseball bat, a hammer, or broom handle you will be wrong.

2. Until you have correctly gripped and re-gripped the golf club over and over with one of the three correct golf grips, the act of correctly placing your hands on the club will feel unnatural and contrived. You are establishing new patterns or, in the case of relearning the grip, breaking old patterns and establishing new patterns at the same time. This will take time.

3. Your brain will not recognize the necessity of the golf-grip motor skill you are adding, and during the cognitive phase of learning you are vulnerable to falling back to some other grip or some combination of grips your brain already has in storage. You must convince your brain that this skill is necessary.

Learning Reminder: In learning motor skills our brains try to match up previously learned motor skills with new skills, and use combinations of old motor skills to expedite the acquiring of new skills. Sometimes this transfer speeds the process, but in doing so the new skill may not be fully or correctly learned. We can use transfer when it benefits us, but we must learn to reject it when it is detrimental to the learning process. So, you have to overcome the natural tendency of your own brain to reject learning the new motor skill and to substitute prior skills. In this case the new grip is a new motor skill. Repetition and visualization are the tools you will use to make your brain comfortable with your new grip and make it an automatic skill, controlled eventually by the cerebellum.

The Three Grips

There is no one grip that is best for every player. Let me emphasize by repeating, there is no one grip that is best for every player. What I will describe here are the correct methods of placing your hands on the club for each grip to achieve "unity" during the swing. This unity will give you the best chance to produce the speed and accuracy you need to successfully control the golf ball. Certain fundamental rules apply to all three grips.

THE VARDON OR
OVERLAPPING GRIP

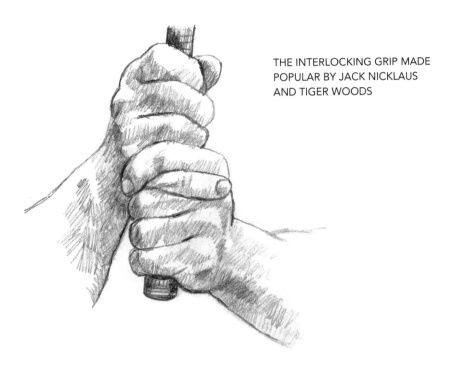

THE INTERLOCKING GRIP MADE
POPULAR BY JACK NICKLAUS
AND TIGER WOODS

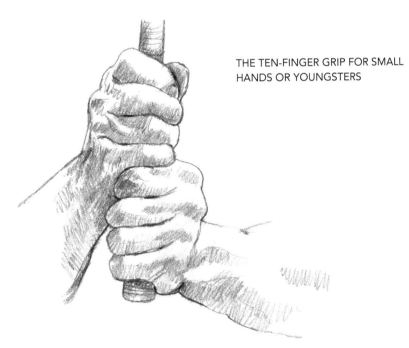

THE TEN-FINGER GRIP FOR SMALL
HANDS OR YOUNGSTERS

The Basics

1. Your hands should oppose each other. The palm of the right hand faces the target and the back of the left hand faces the target. You must maintain this relationship as you grip the club.

2. It is critical that your hands be a unit. There is not a dominant hand in the golf grip. There should be no space between the left and right hands in the completed grip. The hands should fit snugly together.

3. In each grip you will form a V between the forefinger and the thumb of each hand. The left hand V should point to a point on your right shoulder just where your neck meets the shoulder. The right hand V should point to the right shoulder. It is opposite for left handers.

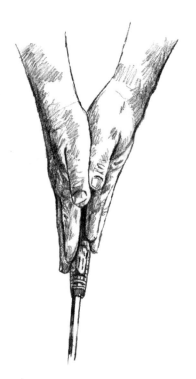

THE HANDS OPPOSE EACH OTHER SO THAT ONE HAND IS NOT MORE DOMINANT THAN THE OTHER.

THE V OF THE RIGHT HAND POINTS TO THE RIGHT SHOULDER. THE V OF THE LEFT HAND POINTS TO THE RIGHT SIDE OF THE NECK

THE LEFT HAND GRIP

The position of the club in the left hand (right hand for lefties) is the same for all three grips.

To correctly position your left hand on the club, start with the club resting on the ground and the face of the club pointing toward the target. The back of the left hand should be facing toward the target and parallel to the sole of the club. Cup the fingers of the left hand in a U shape, and place the grip end of the club in the U shaped groove of the fingers.

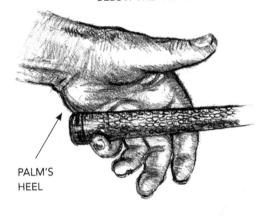

THE CLUB LAYS ACROSS THE FINGERS AND ONTO THE PALM BELOW THE PALM'S HEEL.

PALM'S HEEL

Place your hand around the shaft with your thumb extended down the shaft. The uppermost portion of the grip end of the club will rest under the palm's heel. The last three fingers are the ones that will be doing the work. Leave at least one-half inch of the club extending from your hand in order to maintain proper grip pressure, and test yourself by lifting the club while holding it with the last three fingers of your left hand and the heel pad alone.

THE LAST THREE FINGERS OF THE LEFT HAND PROVIDE THE GRIPPING POWER. NOTICE THE CLUB REMAINS BELOW THE PALM'S HEEL.

Now close your left hand around the club, extending your left thumb down the shaft slightly across the center line of the club and position it at approximately one o'clock. The club now rests across the forefinger and palm of the left hand. Do not let the club extend up on the heel pad of the left hand. If it does, you will not be able to control the club. Not keeping the club under the heel pad is a major grip flaw among amateur golfers. This is what causes the wear point on the golf glove. The thumb of the left hand extends down the shaft and crosses the shaft at 1 o'clock, and will provide a guide for the placement of the right hand.

Look at the V formed by the thumb and forefinger of your left hand. When you stand up to a ball this V should point to a spot where your neck meets your right shoulder. If not, move your grip around the shaft until it does. When the V is properly aligned you have the correct positioning of your left hand. (The left-handed golfer's right hand mirrors this alignment

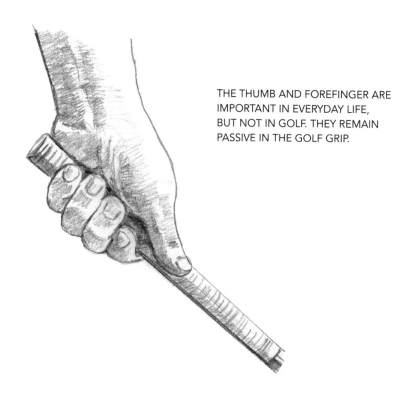

THE THUMB AND FOREFINGER ARE
IMPORTANT IN EVERYDAY LIFE,
BUT NOT IN GOLF. THEY REMAIN
PASSIVE IN THE GOLF GRIP.

for correct positioning and points to where his/her neck meets the left shoulder.).

Now that you have learned to position your left hand, how you choose to position your right hand determines your choice of one of the three grips. There is no preferred grip, but keep in mind that the purpose of the grip is to unify your hands on the golf club. Pick the grip that allows you to accomplish this in the most efficient manner.

THE VARDON OR OVERLAPPING GRIP

The defining feature of this grip is the little finger of the right hand overlaps the forefinger of the left hand.

The Vardon grip or overlapping grip is used by approximately eighty percent of the golfers playing today.

Grip the club as described above in your left hand. Now, place the fingers of the right hand under the shaft. The little finger is wrapped around the forefinger of the left hand. It will settle on or between the forefinger and the second finger. The two middle fingers wrap around

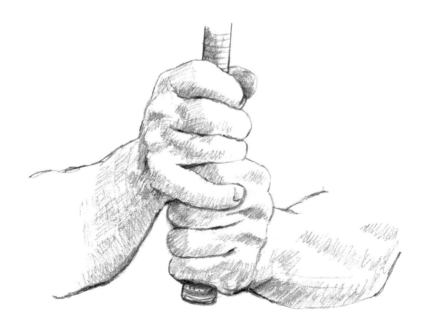

AS YOU PLACE THE RIGHT HAND ON THE CLUB, SLIDE YOUR THIRD FINGER TIGHTLY UP AGAINST THE FOREFINGER OF YOUR LEFT HAND, AND LET YOUR LITTLE FINGER WRAP ON TOP OF YOUR FOREFINGER. YOUR THUMB WILL FORM A NATURAL SADDLE FOR THE V BETWEEN YOUR THUMB AND FOREFINGER TO REST ON AS YOU GRIP THE CLUB. REMEMBER THE GRIPPING FINGERS ARE THE MIDDLE TWO FINGERS; THE THUMB AND FOREFINGER ARE PASSIVE.

the shaft and will meet with or come close to meeting with the thumb of the left hand. If you have too big of a gap between your fingers and your thumb it is an indication that your grips may be too large. This could restrict the natural rotation of the club as you swing through the hitting zone. The two middle fingers provide the gripping power on the club for the right hand.

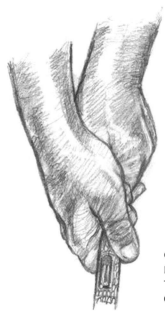

The palm of the hand closes on the thumb of the left hand, which is extended down the shaft at 1 o'clock. The right thumb then extends down the shaft at 11 o'clock closing with the forefinger. The thumb will touch the top of the forefinger lightly.

Take a look at your right hand. There is a V formed by the thumb and forefinger. This V should point to your right shoulder.

CHECK THE COMPLETED GRIP FOR SNUGNESS BETWEEN YOUR HANDS, AND TO ASSURE THAT THE V'S ON BOTH HANDS POINT IN THE CORRECT DIRECTION.

If not, move your grip around the shaft until it does. When the V is properly aligned you have the correct position for your right hand. (The left-handed golfer's left hand mirrors this alignment for correct positioning.)

The V formed by thumb and forefinger on your right hand produces a small cradle that will support the club at the top of your backswing.

INTERLOCKING GRIP

The defining feature of this grip is that the little finger of the right hand is placed between the forefinger and the second finger of the left hand. This grip is used by Tiger Woods and Jack Nicklaus. While it is not the most popular grip, it has been the choice of two of the world's all-time best players.

The first three fingers of the right hand are placed under the shaft. The little finger is simultaneously interlocked with the forefinger of the left hand, while the two middle fingers are wrapped around the shaft and will meet with or come close to meeting with the thumb of the left hand.

AS YOU PLACE THE RIGHT HAND ON THE CLUB SLIDE YOUR THIRD FINGER TIGHTLY UP AGAINST THE FOREFINGER OF YOUR LEFT HAND, AND LET YOUR LITTLE FINGER SLIDE BETWEEN THE FOREFINGER AND SECOND FINGER OF YOUR LEFT HAND. YOUR THUMB WILL PROVIDE A NATURAL SADDLE FOR THE V BETWEEN YOUR THUMB AND FOREFINGER TO REST ON AS YOU GRIP THE CLUB. REMEMBER THE GRIPPING FINGERS ARE THE MIDDLE TWO FINGERS; THE THUMB AND FOREFINGER ARE PASSIVE.

If you have too big of a gap between your fingers and your thumb, it is an indication that your grips may be too large. This could restrict the natural rotation of the club as you swing through the hitting zone. The two middle fingers provide the gripping power for the right hand. The forefinger holds the club in a looser manner. The palm of the hand closes on the thumb of the left hand, which is extended down the shaft at 1 o'clock. The right thumb then extends down the shaft at 11 o'clock and the forefinger closes. The thumb will touch the top of the forefinger lightly.

Take a good look at your right hand. There is a V formed by the thumb and forefinger. This V should point to your right shoulder. If not, move your grip around the shaft until it does. When the V is properly aligned you have the correct positioning of your right hand. (The left- handed golfer's right hand mirrors this alignment for correct positioning.)

The V formed by your right hand produces a small cradle that will support the club at the top of your backswing.

TEN FINGER GRIP

The defining feature of this grip is that it resembles the baseball-bat grip. All eight fingers of the hands are placed on the club. The little finger of the right hand is snugly placed next to the forefinger of the left hand. This grip is primarily recommended for golfers with small hands and children who require more leverage in the hands to control the golf club.

The fingers of the left hand are placed on the club with the V formed by the thumb and forefinger pointing at the right shoulder. The club is held in the fingers of the left hand, and the the finders are placed snugly together. The right hand fingers are placed under the shaft, with the last three fingers wrapped around the shaft and held snugly against the forefinger of the left hand. These three fingers will meet with or come close to meeting with the thumb of the left hand. If you have too big of a gap between your fingers and your thumb it is an indication that your grips may be too large. This could restrict the natural rotation of the club as you swing through the hitting zone. The two middle fingers provide the gripping power for the right hand. The forefinger grips less tightly than the middle two fingers. The palm of the hand closes on the thumb of the left hand, which is extended down the shaft at one o'clock using the life line as a guide. The right thumb then extends down the shaft at eleven o'clock and the forefinger closes. The thumb will touch the top of the forefinger lightly.

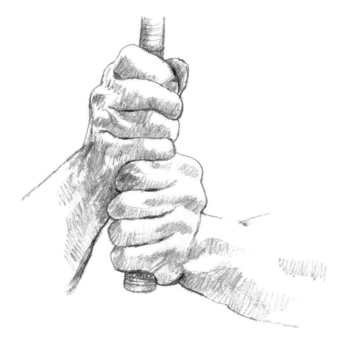

IT IS CRITICAL TO THE TEN-FINGER GRIP
THAT THE HANDS BE KEPT SNUGLY
TOGETHER IN THE FINISHED GRIP.

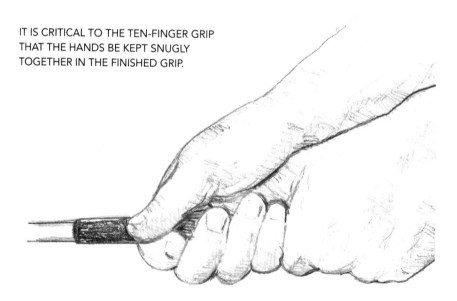

There is a V formed by the thumb and forefinger. This V should point to the outside edge of your right shoulder. If not, move your grip around the shaft until it does. When the V is properly aligned you have the correct positioning of your right hand. (The left-handed golfer's left hand and shoulder mirrors this alignment for correct positioning.)

The V formed by the finger and thumb produces a small cradle that will support the club at the top of your backswing.

General Information

While the thumb and forefinger of the right hand are probably our most useful tools in everyday life, in the golf grip they play a secondary role. Do not let them dominate your golf grip.

The golf club is held by the middle two fingers of the right hand and the last three fingers of the left hand. If we use the forefingers of either hand combined with the thumb we tend to over-grip with that hand, and that side becomes dominant. By utilizing the five fingers, as I have explained, you will develop greater feel around the green, and you will have greater snap in the full swing, creating more speed. Be very careful in forming the left hand grip to keep the club shaft *under* the heel pad. If the club shaft extends up on the heel pad it cannot be locked in place, and you will lose the control you are trying to achieve. I believe allowing the club to extend up on the heel pad is the number one grip fault in golf.

How tight should you hold the golf club? I've heard every answer to that question. Hold it like a bird. Use a certain percentage of your gripping power. Hold like it's a child's hand. I have never heard one that really gave me any idea of what description I could use to consistently describe grip pressure to students. It's easy enough when you are right in front of me to just have you pull my club out of my hand. Then you say, "Wow, that's all the tighter you hold your club?" I say, "Yes," and that's the end of the grip pressure lesson. But, that won't work in a book. Johnny Miller had this to say about the grip:

"Only one golfer in a thousand grips the club lightly enough."

So I am going to explain it like this:

1. Almost all amateurs hold the club too tight.
2. To play the game of golf you need soft (relaxed) hands. If I threw you an unboiled egg, you would need soft hands to catch it.
3. Having too firm of a grip contracts muscles in the forearms and upper arms. This will restrict the smoothness of your swing motion.
4. The tighter you grip the less chance you have to make a proper wrist cock and will restrict your ability to release the wrist cock. You lose distance and accuracy.
5. I have never actually seen anyone lose a club because they were holding the club too loosely.

My recommendation is to take what you believe is a relaxed grip and then loosen up just a bit. Your grip will tighten as you swing the club.

Drills

GRIP STICK: EASY

Sam Snead used a ruler to teach the grip. You can use a ruler or any other flat stick of approximately the same size. Use it to practice your grip when using a golf club would be awkward or inconvenient. Just remember to keep one thumb on each side of the ruler and everything will fall nicely into place.

CLOSET TEST

Take your club into a closet or other dark space and put your full grip on the club. Return to the light and see how you have done. Be sure to check out your alignment V's with the points on your shoulder. Close is not good enough. In between tests give yourself at least thirty minutes before you try again.

LEFT HAND DRILL: (MEDIUM)

This drill will give you a sound understanding and feel for the proper positioning of the club in the left hand. Locking it under the heel pad is the only way to maintain a firm grip throughout this drill.

1. Grip the club (6-iron) in the last three fingers of your left hand while keeping the thumb and forefinger off the club. Be sure to keep the club below the heel pad on the left hand.
2. Raise the club until your forearm is parallel to the ground.
3. Hold for five seconds and lower to the ground.
4. Repeat ten times.

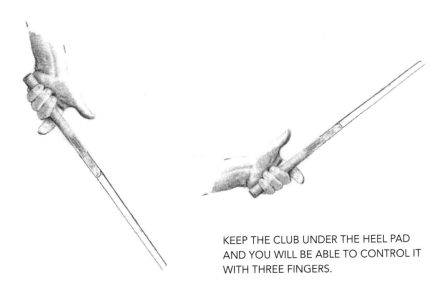

KEEP THE CLUB UNDER THE HEEL PAD AND YOU WILL BE ABLE TO CONTROL IT WITH THREE FINGERS.

SWING DRILL (DIFFICULT)

The purpose of this drill is to learn to control the club with the gripping fingers. The thumb and forefinger of each hand are not to be used to control the golf club.

1. Grip the club (6-iron) using only the last three fingers of your left hand and the middle two fingers of the right hand.
2. Using a short backswing, hit balls.
3. Do not over-swing; just make a smooth swing and concentrate on keeping the correct grip. Check your grip each time you set up.
4. As your confidence grows, let your swing path grow.

If you cannot control the club in this drill, it is an indication that you are hitting at the ball rather than swinging through it.

The Stance

An old Chinese proverb expresses it this way, "I hear and I forget; I see and I remember, I do and I understand."

There is a right and a wrong way to stand in golf. The correct way frees the feet for proper footwork, positions the hips, torso and shoulders for proper rotation, allows the arms to swing freely, and keeps the golfer in balance. An incorrect stance will sacrifice one or more of these important elements, leading to swing errors and errant shots.

In this section we will learn the correct stance or setup position. In the military, uniformity is the key to success. In golf uniformity is not required, but fundamentals are. Everyone is built differently, so your stance may look different from someone else's, but they both can be correct. The key for you as an individual is not to have a different stance each time you get ready to hit the ball. Just like the grip, your stance and its repetition will create consistency in your swing.

The first element in your stance is the placement of your feet. The width of your stance determines the stability of your swing. The bigger the swing arc the more stability you need. This means the longer the club, the wider the stance.

How far apart should your feet be placed? I teach three positions for the feet. I believe that any more positions create too many variables, and variables create opportunities for error. The positions depend on which club you are using.

1. With a driver and teed-up three wood: The width is measured from inside heel to inside heel and is the same width as your shoulders.
2. Fairway woods, rescue clubs, long and mid irons: the width is one shoe width narrower than your driver stance.
3. Short irons: The width is one and one-half shoe widths narrower than your driver stance.
4. The critical point is to be consistent in your stance widths; same stance width, same club, same shot, every time.

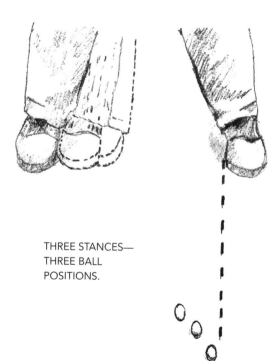

THREE STANCES—
THREE BALL
POSITIONS.

The positioning of your feet prepares your skeletal system for the movement phase of your golf swing. In a neutral stance both feet are perpendicular to and the same distance from the ball-target line. We line up to an imaginary line that runs parallel to the ball-target line. We call this line the alignment line or stance line. The toes of both feet are touching the line; the heel bones, the knee bones, the hip bones and the shoulders are all parallel to this line. You can verify this by placing a golf club across your knees to check if they are parallel to the alignment line and the ball-target line. If you move either foot back or forward of the alignment line, you will not be able to align your skeletal system parallel to the ball-target line.

Note this exception: In order to facilitate a more open turn with the shorter irons you can open the left foot to the target. This can be done after assuming the original position and then pivoting on the heel of the left foot. Turning the left foot out in this manner keeps the heel bones in line and does not affect the alignment of your hips and shoulders.

In the illustration, you see the ball-target line and you see the golfer with a parallel line drawn along his toes. His knees and hips are also aligned with that line. Sometimes it helps to restate fundamentals. We keep our feet perpendicular to the ball-target line. We keep our heels, knees, hips and shoulders parallel with the ball-target line. This gives us the best opportunity to swing our club at the target.

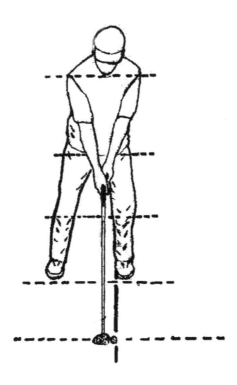

In the stance we want to be balanced; both knees are slightly flexed and they remain so throughout the swing. What does slightly flexed mean? I always say to students, "Get your balance and be in an athletic position." If they are still puzzled I ask them to imagine that they are on the edge of a tall building, and there is a steady breeze blowing and they need to maintain their balance. Immediately they respond by bending their knees and leaning forward, creating a spine angle. This is an athletic position. You can do this easily at home. How much angle do you need? This all depends on your body type and how effectively you produce rotation. You need enough angle so that your arms hang freely in front of your chest, and swing freely so that you are able to rotate around your spine while maintaining that angle. Your setup position will not necessarily look like your friend's.

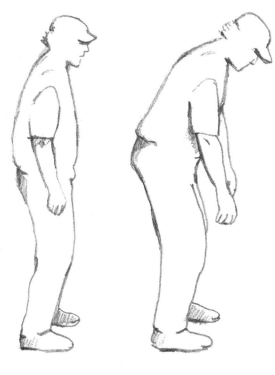
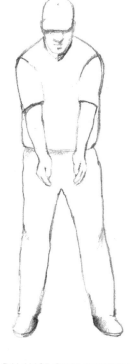

BEND KNEES
SLIGHTLY

BEND AT THE HIPS AND
LET ARMS HANG FREELY

BALANCE ON THE INSIDE
OF BOTH FEET

Swing speed is a function of hip, torso and shoulder rotation. Your balance must be maintained during this movement, and knee flex is a critical element to maintaining this balance. The proper combination of knee flex and spine-angle tilt will allow you to maximize your rotation.

To create the proper spine angle you bend at the hips, not at the waist. The best way to understand this is to straighten your back and push your chest out. Holding this position, bend over to the front. This keeps your back straight and you bend at the hips. Now let yourself relax so that there is a very slight curve in your spine and bend over. You will see that the bend in your body comes from the waist. When we rotate we want our backs to be straight so our spine will rotate from top to bottom. If it is curved it can't rotate freely, and the restricted motion interferes with your golf swing. You keep the back straight to allow for the uninterrupted rotation of the torso, hips and shoulders. Do not tuck your butt under; push it out. Your spine will rotate freely from top to bottom. Select an angle that allows for your arms to hang naturally in front of your body. This creates a platform for the free swing of your arms and hands through the hitting area. We don't want to reach out for the golf ball. Keep your head lifted to allow your left shoulder to rotate under your chin on the backswing.

With your arms relaxed and hanging in front of you, look down and bring your left hand to a position just inside your left thigh with the back of the hand pointing toward the target (right hand for lefties). Now bring your right hand over so that the palms meet. That is the proper position for your hands to be when holding the club. Your hands always start from the same position every time, and this is it. Your shoulders will be parallel to the ball-target line, and the front shoulder will be slightly higher than the back shoulder. Now you are in position to address the ball; the weight should be distributed evenly over the insteps of both feet, and the back knee should be cocked in toward the center. When you cock the back knee in you will lower the back hip slightly, creating spinal tilt away from the ball. This position will aid you in staying behind the ball through contact.

Footwork

"Foot action is one of the main differences between a good golfer and a duffer."

—Sam Snead

There is not a movement sport in the world in which the athlete doesn't get better when his or her footwork improves. We don't hear much about the improvement a golfer makes because of changes in footwork, but believe me it is there. Tougher workout schedules and losing weight make golfers lighter on their feet, and that means better footwork.

In grade school one of the first physical education drills we did was learn to skip. Those of us who could do it just skipped around the circle, more or less amazed by the kids who could not skip. It was a simple drill testing the progress of each child's coordination. There were kids who couldn't skip in first grade, and I imagine that some of them can't skip today. But, you know, no one ever taught us to skip in grade school. They just asked us to do it. If we could, we did, and if we couldn't we didn't. There are a lot of things we don't do well because we weren't taught how, so we taught ourselves. Footwork in golf is probably 95 percent self-taught. Those who do it well learned it as youngsters and so they have the perception that it is easy and really just comes along with the swing. Nothing to it. Those who pick up golf later in life approach footwork with the same attitude—there should be nothing to it. Everything you read is about the swing, so golf must be in the swing. "If I start swinging," the golfer tells himself, "the footwork will follow." Nothing could be farther from the truth.

You can't learn the golf swing if you don't learn the footwork. Period. So learn it, or be prepared to spend time in the woods, purchase a ball retriever, and never own a Pro V, because without proper footwork you're never going to be a consistent golfer. Bad footwork simply ruins everything else you do right.

The transfer of weight to the back foot, and then transferring it again to the front foot at the proper time while maintaining balance, is just as important to your golf game as the simple action of removing your foot from the gas pedal is to slowing down your car. If you drive a car you let up on the gas automatically, but less than ten percent of all golfers transfer weight correctly. That's right, less than ten percent.

Bad footwork is the major cause of the out-to-in swing path. Bad footwork is a major sign of a *hitter* rather than a swinger. Golf footwork becomes easier to understand once you realize that golf is about club-head speed and not about club-head power. Speed is created by rotation of the hips, torso and shoulders, and not by driving laterally off your back foot. This means that you want to be light on your feet, more like a dancer than a football player, as you transfer weight from front to back to front again.

This is the golf swing footwork.

First we need to get a feel for the ground. Without having a feel for the ground you will not have confidence that you can maintain balance throughout your swing. You want to know if the ground is wet or dry, loose or firm, uphill or down. You need to establish what the surface feels like underfoot. When you assume your stance, move your weight from side to side and front to back. Feel the signals from your feet, and then *settle in* with the weight evenly distributed on both feet on level ground. On an uneven surface you will distribute it more to the downhill side. Your balance point is not on your toes, and it is not on your heels, but centered over your insteps. You will now be firmly grounded, and fully capable of making the rotational moves required in the golf swing. Your feet give you stability, but they are not intended to be anchors.

To prepare for the weight shift to the right foot, cock your right knee slightly in toward the center. This serves two functions. First, it will aid in creating tension in your right leg during the rotation of your shoulders, torso and hips to the rear during the takeaway. The release of this tension will automatically shift your weight to the front foot. Second, the cocking of the right knee will assist in lowering the right shoulder.

THE RIGHT KNEE IS BENT IN TO ADD PRESSURE TO THE INSTEP OF THE RIGHT FOOT.

You transfer weight to your back foot by creating downward pressure on your instep—imagine you are squashing a bug. As you begin the takeaway, your weight transfers to the back foot, but there is little lateral motion in your upper body. The down-pressure, along with the rotation, creates tension on the inside of your back leg because weight is on the instep, and your knee is cocked. This position makes it easy to begin the downswing. Before you begin the downswing you release the down-pressure on the instep, and your weight moves to the front foot. The front-foot side controls the rotation of the

AT SET-UP EVEN PRESSURE IS APPLIED TO THE INSIDE OF BOTH FEET. DURING THE
BACKSWING THE DOWN-PRESSURE IS APPLIED TO THE INSIDE OF THE BACK FOOT.
BEFORE THE SWING BEGINS, DOWN-PRESSURE ON THE BACK FOOT IS RELEASED
AND TRANSFERRED TO THE FRONT FOOT. AS THE SWING IS COMPLETED, THE
FRONT FOOT ROLLS OVER, THE WEIGHT GOES TO THE HEEL, AND THE BACK FOOT
RISES TO THE TOE.

swing, and you brace against the instep of the front foot until contact
with the ball. Just as you contact the ball, your front foot rolls over to the
outside and as you complete your rotation, the weight goes to the heel
while your unweighted back foot rises to its toe.

We stay in balance because you control your center of mass by keeping
your weight on your insteps through most of the swing. You start your
swing with your weight evenly distributed. The center of mass is held in
check by the insteps of your feet, and it will remain under control when it
stays inside your stance. When you shift weight to your rear foot by applying
down-pressure, the center of mass moves toward the rear foot. To keep the
center of mass inside your stance you cannot allow the back foot to roll over
to the outside. Trap it with the instep of the back foot. There is now as much
as 80 percent of the body's weight on the back foot, but it must be in balance
and ready to move back to the front. This is accomplished by levering the
back leg inward (or cocking) at the knee when you initially take your stance.
To begin the downswing, the down-pressure on the instep of the back foot
is released and the center of mass shifts back to the front side of the body,
where it is trapped by the instep of the front foot. With 80 percent of the
weight now on the instep of the front foot, the hip rotation begins. The torso
and shoulder rotation follow naturally and the swing will drop into place.
At the bottom of the swing, the front-foot instep releases and the foot rolls
over to the heel with the pivot action of the hips allowing you to maintain
your balance, while the back foot rises to its toe. This footwork keeps the
center of mass under control and at the same time derives any mechanical
advantage it can out of the movement of the center of mass.

FOOTWORK DRILLS

Weight Shift Drill: To learn to control shifting your weight you need to be able to transfer your weight from your left side to your right side and back. We want to keep your center of mass inside our insteps in order to maintain balance. To do this it is important that you can move weight from instep to instep.

Take your stance position; fold your arms across your chest. Your weight should be distributed evenly on both insteps with knees bent. Now cock your right knee in toward the center of your stance about two inches. Without shifting your body, place down-pressure on the instep of the right foot. This will take some practice, but you can learn to do it—imagine squashing a bug under your right instep. Watch yourself in a mirror and do this until you can transfer the weight without making any motion.

Once you can move the weight to the right side in this manner, you will notice that you have created tension in your right leg. If you relax the down-pressure the tension causes the weight to shift toward the front foot. Down-pressure, release, feel the weight shift and relax. Repeat in three-minute sessions.

Weight Shift Drill Two: This is a more advanced drill for practicing footwork. After you have mastered Drill One, this drill adds your arms. Its purpose is teach you to move your weight to the front foot prior to initiating rotation.

Take your stance. Dangle your arms loosely in front of you and join your hands. Transfer your weight to your back foot as you learned in Drill One. In this drill rotate your shoulders, torso and hips to the rear while at the same time you swing your arms shoulder high and stop. Release the down-pressure on your back leg and feel the weight move to the front instep, as you rotate your hips, torso, and shoulders and let your arms follow. Extend your trailing arm out to the front and allow your weight to roll over to the outside edge of your front foot. Repeat in three-minute sessions.

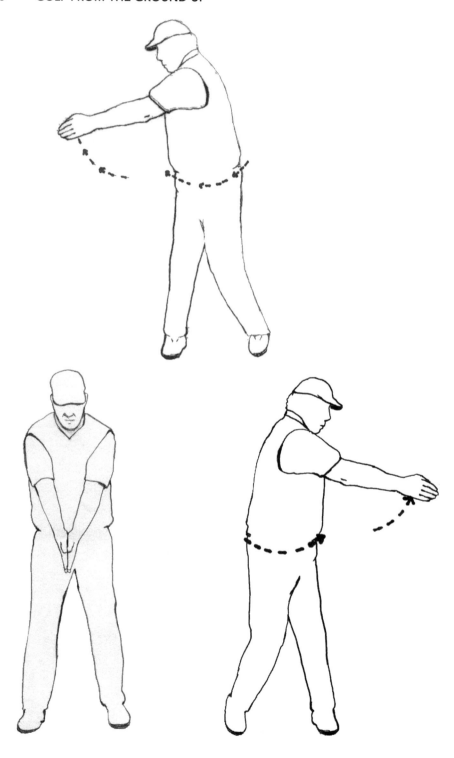

Rotation

Rotation is the engine of the golf swing.

The more time you spend on this section the more you will understand how to develop speed in your golf swing. This is where the swing speed comes from. Surprised? Swing speed does not come from your arms or your wrists or your hands. They function as stabilizers, grippers, and enable you to cock the club. The club-head speed is generated by the rotation of the hips, torso, and shoulders. The left (front) hip is the pivot point where all the rotational movement of the downswing is centered. In order to set up the downswing we need to make a backswing that sets the hands at the same place every time to begin the downswing. If we don't, how can we have the same swing?

In order to accomplish this we use the laws of physics. Starting the golf club in motion with the hands or the arms is asking for trouble and is fundamentally incorrect. The laws of physics tell us that any time we move something there will be resistance. If we start it moving slowly and gradually pick up momentum, we have the best opportunity to move the object in the intended direction. In this case we want to move the golf club away from a ball along the ball-target line. We want to be able to do this time after time on a consistent path so it will end up in the same place at the top of the backswing. If it starts out on the incorrect line, it will be very difficult for us to redirect it to the proper position at the top of the backswing.

The large muscles of the shoulders and back are best suited to start the club away from the ball at a controllable speed and on the correct path. The hands and the arms are controlled by smaller muscles and are not as reliable in making this first move. Using the triangle created by the shoulders, arms, and the joining of the hands, we move the club away from the ball by rotating the shoulders. We can get the club waist-high through the rotation of the shoulders alone. The rotation of the shoulders is the

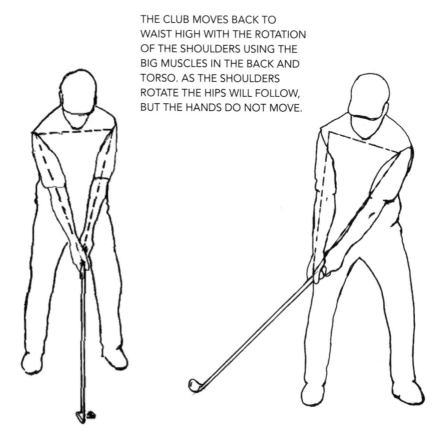

THE CLUB MOVES BACK TO WAIST HIGH WITH THE ROTATION OF THE SHOULDERS USING THE BIG MUSCLES IN THE BACK AND TORSO. AS THE SHOULDERS ROTATE THE HIPS WILL FOLLOW, BUT THE HANDS DO NOT MOVE.

second in the sequence of four steps required for a proper backswing. (The first is the down-pressure on the back foot.) By rotating the shoulders, we also keep the club in front of our chest as it rotates back. As the shoulders rotate the torso rotates and the hips follow. Ideally, we would like the shoulders to rotate 90 degrees to the ball-target line and the hips to follow with 45 degrees. You remember that the right foot has been placed at 90 degrees to the ball-target line to restrict the hip rotation. This restriction of hip rotation creates torque in the back muscles and abdominals during the shoulder rotation. promoting more speed in the downswing.

JUST PAST WAIST HIGH YOU SEE THE ARMS AND WRISTS BECOME INVOLVED AS THE CLUB IS LIFTED AND THE COCKING ACTION BEGINS. AT THE TOP OF THE SWING THE ROTATION IS COMPLETE. THERE IS A 35- TO 45- DEGREE SEPARATION BETWEEN THE SHOULDERS AND HIPS. DOWN-PRESSURE ON THE RIGHT FOOT IS RELEASED AND THE SWING BEGINS WITH THE ROTATION OF THE HIPS.

The sequence shows the shoulders (big muscles) finishing the rotation. Weight is transferred to the inside of the back foot. The hands are now cocked relative to the line of the shoulders. The shoulders have turned while the arms and hands have remained steady, and they are in front of the chest. At waist high the leading edge of the golf club has the same angle as the golfer's spine angle. Notice that the back leg has remained bent and the weight remains on the inside. The chest rotates to the rear while the hands remain centered on the chest. The middle muscles (arms) are starting to raise the club diagonally across the back shoulder, and at the same time the little muscles of the wrists are beginning to cock. At the top of the swing the 90-degree rotation of the shoulders and the 45 degree hip rotation are complete. The legs have remained bent throughout. The right knee is straining to keep its cocked position. Everything is ready to release the downswing.

The downswing is initiated from the ground up. First we relax the down-pressure on the back leg, which shifts the weight to the front foot, and with the left hip acting as the pivot we rotate the hips as fast as we can. Notice I did not say the weight slides to the front; there will be some sideward movement, but do not initiate it. The hip rotation will

THE HIPS HAVE ROTATED PAST SQUARE AND THE SHOULDERS ARE NOT YET SQUARE WITH THE BALL TARGET LINE. THE WEIGHT IS ON THE INSIDE OF THE LEFT FOOT AND THE WRISTS ARE ABOUT TO UNCOCK. THE RIGHT SHOULDER HAS DROPPED DOWN AND IS NOT PUSHED OUT.

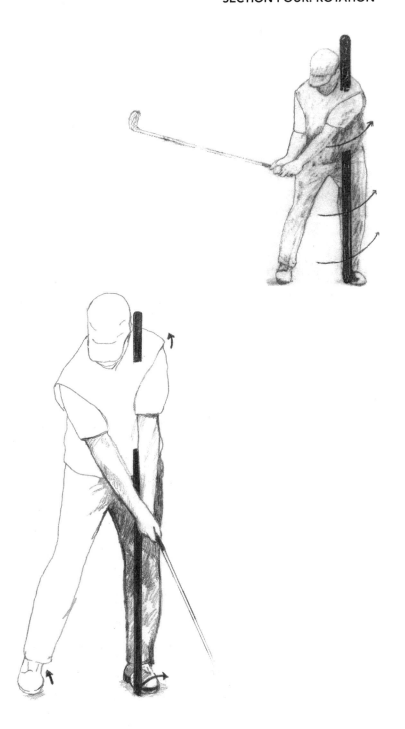

be followed by rotation of the torso, and then the shoulders. The right shoulder does not move out toward the ball-target line and then rotate. Rather, it moves down and rotates, assisting the drop of the arm and the elbow to the inside.

As the body rotates, the left leg and hip pivot, increasing the speed of the swing. In the figures above you see at the moment of impact the hips have rotated past the ball and are open by 45 degrees. The shoulders are aligned with the ball-target line. The sequence is in order. The hips rotated 45 degrees on the backswing (remember you stopped them with your back foot set at 90 degrees to the ball-target line), and the shoulders rotated 90 degrees. On the downswing you fired your hips and they went a full 90 degrees to the front as your front foot rolled over, and your shoulders went 90 degrees as your arms lined up with the ball-target line. Your shoulders continued to rotate in the follow through to catch up with your hips at the finish. The golf swing starts from the ground up in both the backswing and the downswing with the weight shift, but the most obvious motion is the start of the rotation.

1. Weight shift (down-pressure) to the inside of the rear foot begins the golf swing.
2. Keeping your triangle (arms and hands) in front of your shoulders: rotate your shoulders 90 degrees toward the rear. Use the big muscles of the back.
3. Your torso and hips follow the rotation, but stop at 45 degrees, because of your right foot being at a 90-degree angle to the ball-target line.
4. Weight shift (down-pressure) is released from the back foot and moves to the front foot.
5. Your left hip leads the rotation.
6. Your shoulders will follow, with arms and hands remaining in front of your body.
7. Continue the rotation of the hips until you are facing the direction of the target. The shoulders will follow.

Drills

WEIGHT SHIFT AND ROTATE DRILL

The goal of this drill is to put rotation with the footwork.

1. Take your stance
2. Cross both arms across chest
3. Now "squash bugs" under the right instep. (Down-pressure.)
4. Now turn and make a full 90 degree rotation with the shoulders to the back foot; your hips will only rotate 45 degrees .
5. Release the down-pressure; allow the weight to shift to the front side.
6. The forward rotation always begins withs the hips and the torso and shoulders will follow.
7. Repeat ten times.

This drill can also be done with arms hanging loose in front of you. Watch yourself in a mirror to check your body position at setup, at 90 degrees rotation (top of backswing), at contact position, and follow through position (90 degrees to the front). The hips lead the shoulders by 45 degrees through the downswing and the contact point. When your shoulders are parallel to the ball target line, your hips are open 45 degrees. Your shoulders will catch up with your hips at the end or the follow through.

SNAP THE ROTATION

The purpose of this drill is to learn to rotate your hips faster without losing the rhythm necessary to maintain balance and control.

1. Place a tee in the ground.
2. Using a mid-iron, take your normal stance as if you were going to hit a ball from the tee.
3. Close your eyes. (I have you do this so you will swing the club in balance.)

4. Swing as though you were going to hit a ball and clip the tee. Concentrate on snapping the hip around so that your belly button is facing the target.

If you do this drill while maintaining your balance, follow the platform rules and click the tee, you will develop a faster and smoother in-to-out-to-in golf swing.

Ball Position

"Some will never learn anything because they understand everything too soon."

—BLOUNT

Golf clubs are designed to demanding specifications. The golf balls you play with are constructed of the finest materials and tested to give you the highest levels of performance under extreme conditions. Yet most players don't allow the ball and the club the opportunity to get together and show you what they can do. Striking a ball a quarter of an inch off center will reduce the distance it carries by ten percent or more. Just enough, I imagine, to put you in the lake or the bunker on your favorite par three.

The easiest way to prevent this from happening is to establish the correct ball positions and stick with them. You might be thinking, "I've tried a lot of ball positions and none of them works." Or, "I just use what seems to be working today." Let's keep in mind what we are working on here. The platform is a concept that works because the fundamentals work together. Each part contributes to the whole. The placement of the ball is as important to the whole as grip, stance, footwork, rotation, and alignment. Experimentation is done on the practice tee, and change is made only after you are convinced that it is appropriate for your game.

We have been working on a consistent platform. We are doing that to produce a consistent swing. Not thirteen different swings, just one consistent swing. We are doing this so we can know in advance where the bottom of the arc of your swing will be. That is how we know where to place the ball. When you swing the driver and the three wood on the tee box you have a goal in mind. You want to strike the ball just after the bottom of your swing, as the club is on the rise. In your swing path this occurs naturally, at a point directly in front of a line that runs perpendicular from the instep of your left foot to the ball-target line. We are going to call this ball position #1. You will play your driver and teed-up three-wood from ball position #1.

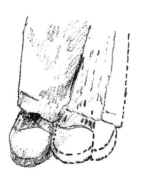

THREE BALL POSITIONS, BUT ONLY ONE HAND POSITION, BECAUSE WE ONLY HAVE ONE SWING.

Next we have a group of clubs that we prefer to sweep from the grass. I call this giving the grass a haircut. These clubs do not take a divot. This place occurs naturally at a point located just one ball back of ball position #1. The clubs you will have the most success playing from here are your fairway woods, and the long and some mid irons. This is ball position #2.

The next group of clubs consists of our short irons. We want to take a divot with these clubs. The position for this club is two balls back from ball position #1. The clubs in this group are your 8-iron through the lob wedge. This is ball position #3.

In each of the ball positions you are hitting different length clubs. The longer clubs require a wider stance. With the driver and teed-up three wood your feet will be shoulder width apart. If you have narrow shoulders and are tall you will want to make this stance wider to give you the stability that you need.

There is nothing complicated about these three ball positions, so quit experimenting and use them to your advantage.

WITH THE LONG IRONS AND FAIRWAY WOODS WE WANT TO SWEEP THE BALL. IT'S CALLED GIVING THE GRASS A HAIRCUT. TO DO THIS WE WANT TO HIT THE BALL AT THE BOTTOM OF OUR SWING. IN OUR SET UP OUR HANDS WILL BE DIRECTLY OVER THE BALL.

FOR OUR SHORT IRONS WE WANT TO TAKE A DIVOT IN ORDER TO ENCOURAGE BACKSPIN. WE WANT TO HIT THE BALL BEFORE THE BOTTOM OF THE SWING. TO DO THIS, IN THE SET UP OUR HANDS ARE IN FRONT OF THE BALL.

WITH THE DRIVER WE WANT TO HIT THE BALL JUST SLIGHTLY ON THE UPSWING. IN OUR SETUP OUR HANDS ARE JUST BEHIND THE BALL.

REMEMBER DURING ALL THIS WE DON'T MOVE OUR HANDS— WE MOVE THE POSITION OF THE BALL.

Alignment

"Whenever a theory appears to you as the only possible one, take this as a sign that you have neither understood the theory nor the problem which it was intended to solve."

—KARL POPPER

Sometimes we waste a perfect shot because we line up incorrectly. If it was a careless mistake, then shame on us. If it was because you lack the skills, then this chapter should give you the information you need to line up correctly.

To hit a golf ball successfully at any target the first task is to establish a ball-target line. The ball-target line is an imaginary line that runs through the ball to the target. We establish our alignment line parallel to that line, and we set up with our feet perpendicular to the alignment line. This sounds easy enough to do, but in real life it's not always that simple.

In Figure 1, the ball-target line is an imaginary line that runs from a point three to five feet behind the ball, through the ball to the target. You should pick out an intermediate target in front of the ball to act as an

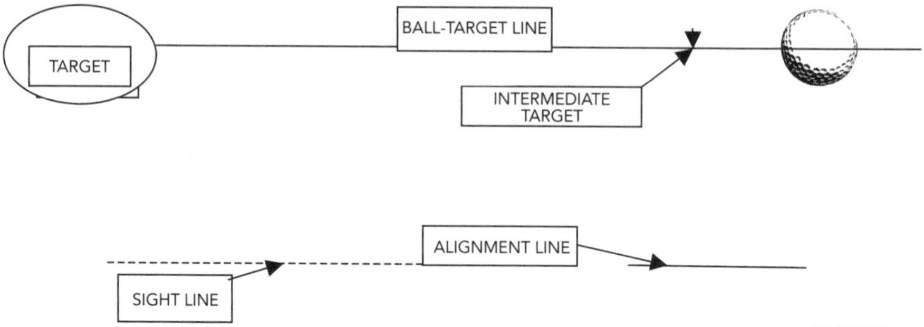

FIGURE 1

aiming point; this intermediate target should be within about three feet of the ball. This can be a leaf, a scuff mark, a divot, a twig or any thing that distinguishes itself from the surrounding area.

You do not want an approximate direction when you pick out the ball-target line. You need to be as exact as you can. This is just one of the many places that a small error can compound itself. A few degrees left or right can mean the difference between missing or hitting the green, the difference between a birdie, a par, or winning or losing. So don't be haphazard; become adept at choosing the intermediate target. The key is to make it as exact as possible.

Your alignment line runs parallel to the ball-target line. When you line up to that line it will appear to you that you are looking left of the target. The farther away from target you are, the further left it will appear you are aiming. This is natural. Do not succumb to the urge to adjust your stance and line up on a line that runs to the target. This will only change your swing path to the right of the target. Remember: the image you are looking at is in the distance and the three-foot parallel line has diverged into a greater width.

Convergence and divergence: two words with opposite meanings, but they do explain why some golfers have a very hard time understanding how to line up. I've tried to explain this concept too many times and sometimes it's like talking about a black hole in space, and I don't want to go there. My son and daughter-in-law are physicists, and they can talk about that stuff, and I just end up giving them the nine-mile stare, so I know what that looks like and feels like. I don't want that to happen here.

We can all line up parallel to another line. And we can see the two lines disappearing in the distance. Conceptually we can think of railroad tracks, and lots of golf books show the railroad tracks leading toward the golf hole. We know from experience that the railroad tracks look like they converge into one out in the distance. We can even verify that phenomenon ourselves if we have a long stretch of track somewhere to look at. They appear to converge.

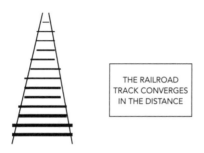

THE RAILROAD TRACK CONVERGES IN THE DISTANCE

Here is the problem: If I tell you to line up parallel to the target line without any explanation, there is a very good chance you will line up parallel and then look at the target and see that you are visually aimed way to the left. Your sight line does not converge like the railroad track in the drawing does, and it never will. This visual image is playing tricks on you. You will adjust your stance line to line up on a line that will converge with the target, like the railroad track drawing. When you do this, you will no longer be aligned on a line that runs parallel to the ball-target line. You are now aiming to the right of the target. The simple fact is that the parallel line (your alignment line) visually diverges from the target when we look up from it. It runs to the left side of the target, and it actually gets farther away (diverges) from the target the farther you extend it. Until you get comfortable with this picture, you will feel like you are lined up way to the left of the target.

A simple way to prove this to yourself is to look out a window. Pick one that is about thirty inches wide and sit about six feet away from the window. The right side is your ball-target line and the left is your stance or alignment line. When you look out the window across your yard to the back fence you will see more than 30 inches of fence, and as you look off into the distance the landscape grows. Remember this the next time you are tempted to realign your setup. The alignment line represents the left side of your field of vision as you looked out the window. It will diverge from the target as the distance to the target increases. We want to swing along the ball-target line.

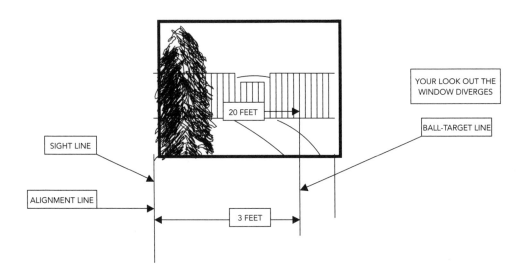

Alignment is something that you really have to practice until it becomes second nature. And then it is something that becomes part of your routine. Ask yourself right now if you understand the elements of the alignment chapter. If you don't then I suggest that you reread the chapter. Every section in the platform is critical to your building a repeatable golf swing, and getting any part of the platform only partly right will give you unsatisfactory results.

ALIGNMENT DRILLS

To work on your alignment you need three golf clubs and a ball. Place the ball on the ground and move behind it. Pick out your target and an intermediate target. We will approach this ball as if it was in the fairway, but it would make no difference if it was on the tee. We would approach it just the same.

1. Determine the ball-target line.
2. Lay one of the golf clubs along the ball-target line.
3. Use the second club to establish the stance line. It should be parallel to the ball-target line.
4. Line your feet up on the stance line, and take your stance.
5. Use the third club to check the alignment of your knees, your hips and your shoulders. Make sure that they are parallel with the stance line.
6. Repeat taking your stance until you are comfortable checking your alignment without the aid of the golf clubs.

The Pre-Shot Routine

"If we are to achieve results never before accomplished, we must employ methods never before attempted."

—Francis Bacon

We have talked about a number of fundamentals that will help you be a better golfer without working on your golf swing. They won't work if you can't take them to the course with you every time you play. The best way to do this is the method the professionals use, and it is called a pre-shot routine. Almost everything we have discussed can become a part of your pre-shot routine. Eventually it will become so ingrained that you won't have to think about it; you will just do all of it in order each time you approach a shot. So let's start at the beginning.

As you approach the ball, look around and determine the slope of the ground. Ask yourself these questions: Is it uphill, downhill, side hill? Is it wet, dry? Is the grass long or short? What kind of grass is it? Where is the sun? Is the grass lying in the direction I am striking the ball or against me? Is the wind blowing on this hole? How much? Which direction? In short, you want to gather as much information as you can that will have an effect on the shot you will make. This will determine your choice of club and type of shot. You should be working on most of these questions on your way to the ball. When you have all your information, then you make a club selection.

Stand behind the ball and choose an intermediate target on your ball-target line. Walk to a position parallel to the ball-target line, but before taking your stance over the ball and aligning yourself, there are a couple of physiological and psychological needs that you should take care of. Take some practice swings—not get-loose swings, but swings that you would use to actually hit the ball to the green. If you are not happy with these swings, take more until you find the one that will hit the ball to the green. Second, we all deal in different ways with the fear of failure. One of the body's reactions to the physical component of fear causes the brain to shut off blood supply to the capillaries. One way we can help counteract this is to make certain that we have supplied our blood system with as much oxygen as possible prior to performing the task. Slowly take three or four deep belly breaths while you are studying your ball-target line as you take your stance.

As you settle into your stance, check yourself to make sure you have the proper alignment and that the ball is in the proper place for the club you are hitting. Check to make sure your hands are going to be starting in the right place for the takeaway, and relax your grip. Keep your feet moving. A little pressure here and change of pressure there—don't become a statue. Make sure you have your right knee cocked in toward the center of your stance. If you have developed a waggle with the club that's okay, just remember to quiet the hands when you begin the takeaway.

When you are confident that you have done all that you can do in your conscious mind to prepare for this golf shot, you are ready to begin your personal ritual.

The ritual is a process that shuts down your conscious thought and allows your subconscious to take over. The golf swing takes about one second—one and a half at the most. During that time there are thousands of commands going to your muscles from your brain. You have to trust that your brain knows how to do this best. Being positive about the outcome is the best help you can be to your brain. The orders your brain will give out will be happening at the rate of one-two-hundredths of a second. That's way too fast for us to have any conscious influence over. We may believe that swing thoughts control outcomes, but at this juncture they will just get in the way of what your brain is about to do.

Once the swing starts in motion you can't direct it; you can only wreck it. So relax and trust it.

Now, let's get back to the ritual. When I am set to swing I say to myself, "Trust your swing." Sometime between the words *trust* and *swing*, my swing just goes off automatically. To make this work you have to practice using the ritual. Then it becomes part of your routine. I've been asked, "What happens if your swing doesn't go off while you say the ritual?" Don't worry, it always does.

You can use whatever key words you want for your ritual, but you have to work them into your practice, and you have to use them all the time. They don't help if you use them only when you are in trouble or hitting off the first tee at the club tournament.

So use your routine and your thinking brain to prepare yourself to hit the ball, and then use your ritual to get your thinking brain out of the way while you do it.

3

The
Swing

"Every accomplishment starts with the decision to try."

—U<small>NKNOWN</small>

What is the golf swing? Is it the magical combination of tempo and coordination coming from a knowledge of secret moves that only a very few can master? Are those who possess this knowledge sworn to a lifetime of secrecy? If so, lock your doors and pull the shades because you are about to learn it all. And, if you are willing to spend the time and effort you can learn a swing that is productive, fundamentally correct, and seemingly effortless. I can only promise you that it can happen and not that it will. The swing will not appear overnight, and it will not be yours without a lot of hard work, but if you combine what you will learn in this chapter with the *platform* there will be no one in your way but yourself.

The first secret is that you have to learn only one golf swing. I talked about that earlier and that's right, only one swing. You remember in the section on stance we learned to position our hands in the same place every time. There is a reason for that position. It is the starting place for every swing. We have set positions for the ball. We couldn't do that unless we had a repeatable swing, and a repeatable swing is the same swing. That means that each swing is like the one that went before. Every full swing will start in the same place, and you will take your hands to the same place at the top of the swing with the same cocking action, and you will bring it down the same way and release the wrist cock the same way every time. You will swing exactly the same for every club, and you will learn to rely on your golf clubs to produce different distances, trajectories and spins.

Every golfer has a swing tempo. The tempo is the time the swing takes for you to move the club away from the ball to the top of the swing and back to the ball again. Since the swing is the same for every club, the tempo is the same for every club. *Your swing tempo is unique to you.* Your hands start in the same place for every club and go to the same place at the top of the backswing and end up in the same hitting position. Average tempo on the tour has been measured at around one second. That is not a goal to attain; it is just to give you some idea of what the tempo is on the tour. Your tempo could be slightly faster or as much as a half-second slower.

Every golf swing has a plane or a route that it follows. This is true both of the backswing and the downswing. How you set up to the ball establishes the angle of your plane. As you rotate while maintaining your stance, it is your shoulders and your arms with the club that create a plane around the core of your body. Your reaching left arm will keep the club extended throughout, and the club head will remain in front of your body as you rotate. Your stance will determine whether you are an upright-plane swinger, a flat-plane swinger or somewhere in between. There are advantages to each type.

The upright-plane takes the swing back up over the shoulder on the backswing and has steep path back to the ball. The flat plane takes the club just outside the shoulder and across the back. In both cases the leading edge of the club will parallel to the left forearm at the top of the swing.

The upright swinger will remain in the hitting zone for a longer period because the arc is steeper. Because of this the golfer will have more control

THE ARROW SHOWS THE UPRIGHT
PLANE OF THIS GOLFER'S SWING.

THE GOLFER'S STANCE WILL PRODUCE
A FLATTER SWING PLANE.

of the shots. The upright plane is harder to master because the rotational movement of your hips and torso is not in the same plane with your shoulder rotation.

The flat-plane swinger rotates his torso and hips and shoulders in the same plane, making it easier to cooridinate and utilize the speed developed by the rotation of the hips. The flat plane is easier to learn, and for the average golfer it will impart more swing speed. The downside is that the golfer is in the hitting zone for slightly less time because of the shallow arc of the swing. This causes slightly less control.

What I recommend is that you learn all the elements of the platform and choose a swing that fits your body type. That will make you a solid golfer.

Much of what we know about the golf swing comes from physics. Not real exciting stuff, but understanding the physics principles involved in the design of the clubs helps our thinking. It becomes clear why we use the same swing with every club. The clubs are designed with different lengths and have different lofts and different lies. This is what allows the golfer to use one swing with the same velocity and achieve different results. The golfer must take the club head away (the backswing) and return the club head (the downswing) in such a manner that it can be repeated over and over with little or no variation. To deliver the desired velocity and the correct ball flight to the ball, the club head must be delivered to the ball with the clubface square at impact. This means that the face of the club cannot be open or closed, or have its loft or lie altered at the time of contact with the ball.

The golf swing must be repeatable to avoid mistakes, and the first step to making something repeatable is to make it uncomplicated. In the Marine Corps, where mistakes cost lives, we were taught the acronym, KISS (Keep It Simple Stupid). That's good advice for your golf game. The swing fundamentals are not complicated, but some people try to make

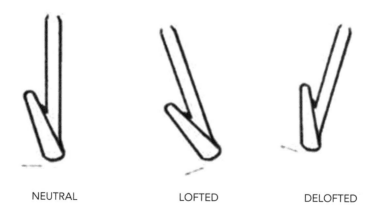

NEUTRAL   LOFTED   DELOFTED

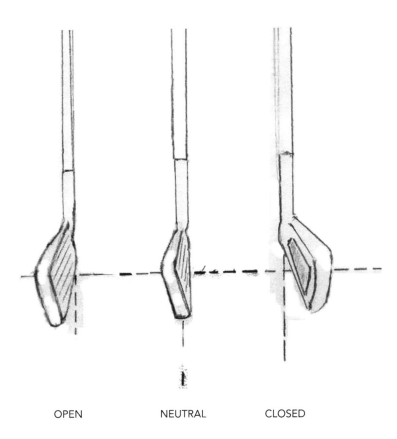

OPEN   NEUTRAL   CLOSED

them complicated. I think that much of what has been written about the swing has done more to confuse golfers than to help them learn what the golf swing is really about.

Most golfers think of the golf swing as one big arc, or pendulum. In fact the golf swing is made up of two pendulums, which without the help of the rotation of our body would swing in two different directions. The first pendulum is the **arm pendulum**. The arm pendulum has its center point on our left shoulder and is scribed by the left arm until just after you strike the ball, at which time the center point of that pendulum transfers to your right shoulder as the right arm straightens and extends out along the ball-target line while the left arm folds.

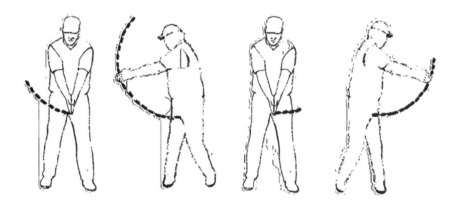

THERE ARE TWO TIMES IN THE SWING WHEN BOTH ARMS ARE EXTENDED AT THE SAME TIME. THE FIRST IS IN THE BACK SWING. THE LEFT ARM REMAINS EXTENDED UNTIL THE CLUB PASSES WAIST HIGH. THIS EXTENDS YOUR ARC AND REMINDS YOU TO KEEP THE CLUB IN FRONT OF YOUR CHEST. THE ARMS EXTEND TOGETHER ONCE AGAIN JUST AFTER CONTACT WITH THE BALL. THIS EXTENSION KEEPS YOUR CLUB HEAD ON THE BALL TARGET LINE AND PREVENTS YOU FROM SWINGING AROUND YOURSELF.

In the arm pendulum one arm is always extended. This allows for the maximum swing arc. Extended does not mean stiff. I prefer to think of the arm in a reaching position. The muscles remain active, and the elbow is not locked. The left arm is the extended arm in the backswing and remains extended in the downswing through contact. Just past contact there is a brief period where both arms are extended, and then the right arm takes over. There is a real reaching or extension movement as club head follows the target line for as long as possible. This extension of the arms during the golf swing is an essential component of the golf swing. But remember, it is one arm at a time except for a brief period right after contact.

The right arm acts as a stabilizer and has just one function. It must guide and help lift the left arm to the same position at the top of the swing on a consistent basis in order for the golfer to develop a repeatable swing. If you don't start down from the same position at the top every time, your pendulum will not be on same plane as it descends toward the ball-target line. The position at the top is critical. This is why we don't reach back for extra distance, because more than likely the result will be to take our swing off plane (usually outside) and the result is a ball that we play from the rough or can't find. When I say reach back, I am talking about those times when we want just a little more distance. The natural thing to do is to try and increase the length of our backswing, so we take our hands just a little higher than ususal. This will result in dipping past parallel and more than likely taking the club head inside of the target. When we reach back we also move our right shoulder up and back, which makes it difficult for us to lower it (or drop) along the same path—which it must do in the downswing in order to keep on the same plane.

The second pendulum is the **wrist pendulum**. The wrist begins cocking the club as the club head moves past waist-high. The center point of the arc is at your wrists. This pendulum is generally referred to as the wrist cock, and actually would move in a different direction than the arm pendulum if it were not for the rotation of your body. If you don't understand this take your stance and cock your wrists. You will see the club move out, up and away from you.

AS YOU COCK YOUR WRISTS THE CLUB MOVES OUT AWAY FROM YOUR BODY.

PREPARATION FOR THE SECOND PENDULUM BEGINS

AS YOU COCK YOUR WRISTS.

In the golf swing the rotation by the shoulders followed by the torso and hips in the backswing sets up the downswing. The shoulders must be turned 90 degrees to the rear to make it possible for the wrist pendulum (cocking of the wrists) to swing in line with the swing of the arm pendulum. If you learn the correct way to release the down-pressure on your rear foot and allow the weight to move to the front foot and rotate your hips, the timing of the downswing and the uncocking of the wrists will happen automatically. The two separate swing arcs combine with the rotation of your hips, torso, and shoulders into the one big arc you usually think of as the golf swing. The less physically and mentally involved you are in the swing, the better your swing will be. There is a physics theory that capturing the kinetic energy by combining the swing arcs correctly is the secret of the golf swing. This makes it possible to swing easy and achieve a high club-head speed.

Physics also explains why the same swing can produce different results. The heads of the longer clubs will be traveling at higher speeds because they are farther away from center of the radius of the swing arc. No additional effort is necessary on the golfer's part to produce this higher swing speed. This additional club-head speed will produce additional distance.

The faces of the clubs have different lofts. The lofts on the clubfaces cause the balls to rise and the dimples cause them to spin, which also causes them to rise. This loft, combined with a shorter club, controls the distance. You make the same swing, and yet your ball does something totally different with an 8 iron than it does with a 3 wood.

Physics also explains why we hit balls that hook and slice. When you cut across the ball-target line with your swing path you put side spin on the ball, which makes the ball either hook or slice. We will discuss more on this in ball flight rules.

Physics provides us the answer to an age-old problem, the out-to-in swing path. You can avoid this problem from the start if you understand the swing and how it works. The arc of the arm pendulum is controlled by

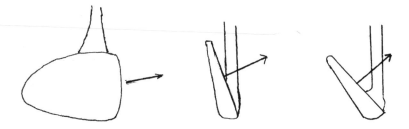

your left arm from the top of the backswing through contact with the ball, with the right arm acting as a stabilizer. To deliver maximum swing speed and repeatability the ideal swing path is in-to-out-to-in. This means that the swing arc travels through the hitting zone as depicted in Figure A. More than 90 percent of golfers swing through the hitting zone with a swing arc as depicted in Figure B.

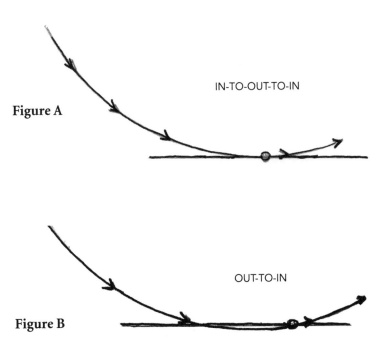

IN-TO-OUT-TO-IN

Figure A

OUT-TO-IN

Figure B

To keep this combined pendulum on an in-to-out-to-in path you must transfer your weight to your front foot **before** you begin the downswing. The consequences for not making this weight transfer will be an out-to-in swing path.

The critical time during the downswing for the wrist pendulum is about waist-high when your shoulders are still 30–40 degees turned away from the ball-target line. If you have not rotated sufficiently on the backswing to achieve this position (on the backswing we must rotate a full 90 degrees to the rear with our shoulders), or if your wrists do not begin to uncock at this time, the club head will move outside and cross the ball target line from out-to-in, causing a slice or a pull. This uncocking happens naturally in the golf swing. If you force it, or incorrectly begin your swing with your hands (also known as "hitting over the top" or casting) you will not drop your right shoulder and arm, and you will throw the head of the club outside of the arm pendulum or plane from the beginning of the swing.

The Difference Between a Hit and a Swing

This may seem like a strange topic, but whenever I watch golfers I divide them into two categories: hitters and swingers. What I am doing here is trying to explain the difference between the two.

A hit has a target and concentrates on the ball; because of this, it can be off target and it loses energy when it strikes the ball. A swing has a path, and concentrates on direction so it continues its energy and direction through the ball. This process results in more energy transferred to the ball and more consistency in the direction. A hit begins in the arms and hands and works its way quickly through the club to the ball; the hands in particular are controlled by small muscles and prone to error. The swing starts in the feet and works its way up through the body, allowing rotation of the hips, torso and shoulders to provide the acceleration. The arms and hands play a passive role, allowing the club head to swing through the hitting zone. This reduces errors. The ball is important to a hit. The ball is not important to a swing. When you hit at the ball you lose as much as ten miles per hour of club-head speed the instant you make contact. This will rob you of distance. Swinging through the ball adds distance and ball control. Jack Burke, Sr. said it best:

"Let the ball get in the way of the swing, instead of making the ball the object of the swing."

So, what does a swing feel like? I think a good description would be the feeling you had on the swings when you played in the park. When you sat on that park swing you developed a feel for direction change and momentum build as you continued through from top to bottom to top. In the golf swing there is a direction change and momentum build as you continue from the top of the backswing through the downswing and to the finish. In the park swing you waited for the backward momentum change at the top of the "backward swinging direction," and you let yourself fall (change direction) before you began to pump. The best park swingers recognized this change and with perfect timing could take their swings high in just a few pumps. The swinging action was effortless. The pumping action came from the hips, the torso, the shoulders, and they used their arms and hands just to hold on. They worked with the momentum of the fall as they pumped to create the effortless swinging action.

So it is with all good golfers. The change of direction at the top of the swing and momentum in the downswing seem effortless to the untrained eye. This effortless swing is a result of combining the drop of the arms into the swing and uncocking the wrists with the momentum created by the rotation of the hips, torso and shoulders. The ball leaves at a velocity that seems unwarranted by the effort. If we pay attention to how this momentum is built we will learn to swing and not to hit.

The mechanics are relatively easy. The arms, especially the forearms and the hands, must remain passive during the takeaway and the direction change. The wrists get involved in cocking and uncocking the club, but it can be said that both of these actions will happen almost "on their own" if you allow them to. It's when you get involved that you get in trouble. Get out of your own way and let the swing happen.

In chapter two we learned the platform and in this chapter we will attach a swing to the platform. The platform fundamentals, except ball position and the width of the stance, remain the same for each golf club. What I will do is explain in general the fundamentals of the swing for the backswing first. The fundamentals of the swing will be the same for all clubs.

The Swing

Step One: Take your stance with the mid-iron of your choice and make sure you have your right knee cocked in toward the center and your weight distributed evenly but focused on the right foot toward the instep. To begin the backswing shift your weight to the right foot by focusing down-pressure on the instep. There is a triangle created by the shoulders and arms by the joining of the hands. Keep this triangle intact and your hands in front of your body while you move the club away from the ball by rotating the large muscles of the shoulders. Your torso and hips follow.

You will be able to get the club waist high or higher through this rotation of the shoulders to about 90 degrees away from the target. Your shoulders are now at an angle that is perpendicular to the ball-target line, and the club is still in front of your chest and waist high. At this point look at the clubface and the leading edge of the club. The angle of the leading edge of the club (bottom edge) will match the angle of the top of your left forearm. If it doesn't you are rotating your hands in the takeaway. This relationship remains constant throughout the golf swing (from setup to follow-through). Your center of mass remains inside your stance. We keep the right knee cocked in and our weight is trapped by the instep of our right foot. This first part of the backswing is the big muscle movement.

If you master Step One and practice it regularly, you will always be able to get off the tee in those situations where muscles tighten up and your mouth goes dry. You will be relying on the big muscles of your body to get your swing stared. Those big muscles perform well under pressure,

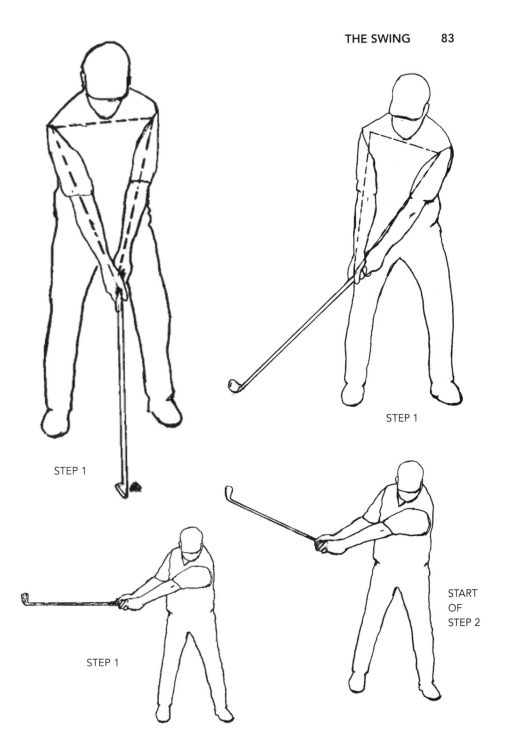

STEP 1

STEP 1

STEP 1

START
OF
STEP 2

KEEP YOUR TRIANGLE, KEEP YOUR HANDS STILL, AND KEEP YOUR CLUB IN FRONT OF YOUR CHEST.

and once you get your swing started back on a reliable path it becomes almost automatic. Start it wrong, and you have no chance.

Steps Two and Three: We now use our middle muscles in our arms to lift our hands up over our right shoulder while maintaining a reaching left arm. At the same time you will begin the wrist cock, using your small muscles. This is the also the start of the second pendulum. When you cock the club the face of the club will remain square to the ball-target line (the leading edge will still match your left forearm). The cocking movement only elevates the club vertically from the ball-target line. Because of the backswing and the golfer's body rotation the toe of the club will end up pointing in a downward direction rather than up. The face of the club will be pointed toward the inside of the swing arc. When the club is cocked in this manner and the face remains square, the wrists can release naturally in the downswing. The wrists will return the hands to a neutral position, making contact with the ball and causing no negative effect on the ball flight. You do not have to manipulate this release. I guess this is what you would call swing magic. When your left arm starts to bend, stop. This is as far as you should take your backswing. How far you reach will depend on your flexibility. Your right arm will be bent with the leading edge of the golf club matching the top of your left forearm.

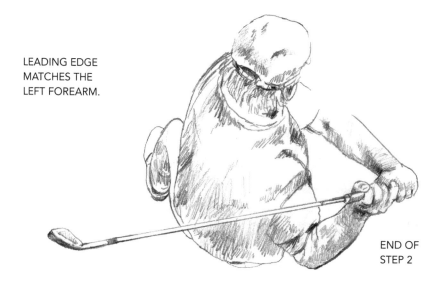

LEADING EDGE
MATCHES THE
LEFT FOREARM.

END OF
STEP 2

The Downswing: The first move of the downswing starts *from the ground up*. Release the down-pressure on the right leg and your legs shift your weight to the front foot. We reverse the motion of the club by uncoiling the muscles of the hips, torso and shoulders. The club will be rerouted down (not out) as you rotate and drop your right shoulder and arm toward your side. Just like pumping a park swing, you have to learn the feel of the downswing. Some will learn it better than others. As you learn to swing, let your arms, wrists and hands be passive and allow the club head to uncock naturally and square itself just before contact. It's only when you learn to feel that downswing happening time after time that you can join in. Remember to keep your arms and hands in front of your body throughout the downswing.

Your shoulder rotation must remain behind your hip rotation by 45 degrees in order for your swing to line up with the ball-target line. The center point of the swing arc or pendulum is the left shoulder. The right arm remains slightly bent and continues to act as a stabilizer as the arms deliver the club to a position inside the ball-target line. The front leg braces against the instep of the front foot.

The swing doesn't end at impact; you extend through impact with your left arm straight. Both arms will be straight at the same time just past the contact point. Then the left arm bends as your right arm extends along the target line as far as you can reach. Exaggerate the feeling—the longer you stay on that target line with your follow-through, the more

START OF STEP 3

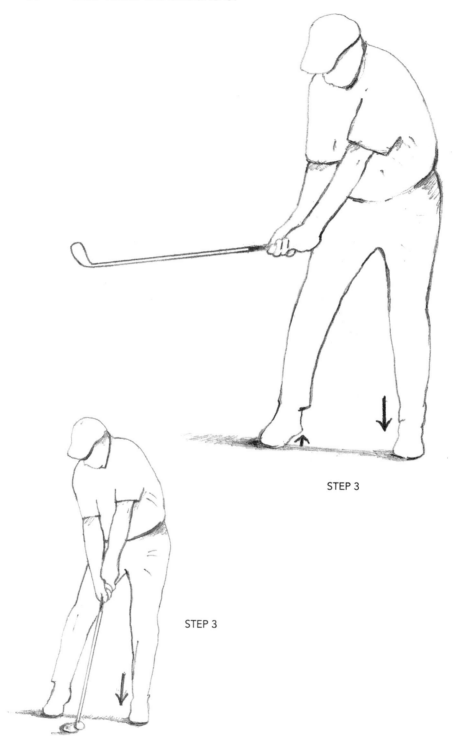

STEP 3

STEP 3

STEP 4—THE FINISH

accurate you will be. Your left arm folds in a mirror image of your right arm in the backswing. Do not wrap your arms and the club around your body. Extend them out, up, and over your left shoulder.

Let me emphasize that the hands serve one function during the golf swing and that is to hold the golf club. We do not roll the hands (supination or pronation) or cup our wrists (flexion or extension) prior to contact with the ball. The clubface does seem to change position as we make our backswing and downswing. There is no real magic; this change happens because of the rotation of our shoulders, torso and hips, and

the cocking of our wrists and the reverse coming down. However, the face of the club remains square to the target line throughout because the hands do not move.

Thoughts on the swing:

1. The grip and starting position for your hands are the same for every swing.
2. When you set up, cock your right knee in toward the middle of your stance, and keep your weight on the insteps of your feet.
3. Footwork, footwork, footwork; transfer your weight to the instep of the back foot at the start of the backswing by applying down-pressure.
4. Release the down-pressure to begin downswing.
5. The triangle formed by your hands on the club, arms, and shoulders should be maintained in the takeaway until your left arm passes waist-high. This will help keep your hands in front of your body where they belong.
6. Keep your hands relaxed but firm during the takeaway; do not cock, break, or roll. When your hands reach waist-high in your backswing it is time to begin to cock. In general they will do this naturally.
7. Position at the top is important. Do not take your club past horizontal. Keep your hands firm.
8. Proper rotation is more important than the length of the backswing when it comes to the speed of the club head at impact. Concentrate on a full 90 degree shoulder rotation.

9. Tempo should be the same for all swings. No different for your driver or your full wedge. Tempo is the time from takeaway to ball contact.

10. Release the down-pressure in your right leg during the wrist cock; this shifts the weight to the front foot and prepares you for the downswing.

11. Keep your grip light throughout the swing and finish out toward the target with a right arm extension.

12. Keep your left knee slightly bent until after contact.

13. Don't go looking for swing problems; check out your platform first.

THE ELBOW SWING DRILL

The purpose of this drill is to acquaint you with the role of the body's rotation in the golf swing. Use a 6-iron and take your normal stance and address the ball in its normal position.

1. Pin your elbows to your sides and keep them pinned there throughout this drill.

2. Use the rotation of your hips, torso and shoulders to swing the club, and hit golf balls. In the backswing make a wrist cock.

3. Do not allow your elbows to release from the side of your body.

4. Make your normal weight transfer and rotate from the hips up.

5. Strike the balls and release out to the target.

THE TAKEAWAY DRILL

The purpose of this drill is to develop a consistent takeaway.

1. Using a five-iron, set up in your normal stance.
2. When we want to start a body in motion we use our largest muscles. In this case it will be the muscles of the shoulders. Concentrate on the middle of your shoulders.
3. Your weight shifts to the instep of your back foot.
4. Rotate your shoulders 90 degrees to your back side while maintaining your setup triangle (hands, arms and shoulders).
5. Keep your hands in front of you at all times, and when your club reaches waist high look to see that the leading edge of the club matches your spine angle.
6. Rotate 90 degrees on your back foot toward the club and set the club back down. You should be in your set up position again.
7. Repeat. Complete the circle three or four times.

LEFT FOOT DRILL

You will need a bucket of balls, a pitching wedge, 8-iron, 6-iron, 4-iron (rescue-club), three wood, and driver. What I want you to understand from this drill is that your swing does not go out-to-in. Your current swing arc is crossing the ball-target line from the outside only because you are late in transferring your weight to your front foot. When you have your weight in the correct place your swing path is in the right place.

1. Set up in a square stance (both feet parallel to the ball-target line) and place 80–90 percent of your weight on the front foot.
2. Address the ball on the inside edge of your front foot.
3. I want you to pay close attention to your takeaway. Make your normal rotation. Your shoulders should make a 90 degree rotation. Stop the club waist high. The leading edge of the club should match your spine angle.
4. Practice this takeaway a couple of times.
5. Now, hit the ball. You should experience a crisp shot, and the club will have approached the ball from the inside.

When you get to the three wood, choke down on the club to the bottom of the grip for the first 5 balls, then hit 5 full length. Repeat that process with the driver (use a tee).

STEP AND SWING

The goal of this drill is to establish a distinction between the weight shift and the beginning of the downswing. You will learn to transfer the weight to your front foot before you begin the downswing. This will happen because you will have to step before you hit the ball. In this drill it is important to work up and down the bag. Starting with your highest lofted club, and changing after each swing. The changing of the clubs before each shot is random practice and causes your brain to rethink before each shot.

This is proven to be the most effective learning technique. Remember to swing, don't hit.

1. Place the ball in its normal set up position.
2. Stand with both feet together where you would normally place your back foot.
3. Take a normal (as possible) backswing and stride forward to hit the ball. Plant the front foot before you swing.

Don't be sloppy about this. Pick out targets and attempt to hit the ball to those targets. The only difference in your setup is the position of your left foot. What we are trying to learn is moving the weight forward. Do not forget the rotation of your shoulders in your backswing.

COCKING DRILL

The purpose of this drill is to limit the looseness players get at the top of the backswing. By making the wrist cock at the start of the swing you will get familiar with a new position at the top of your swing, one that does not dip or cross the line.

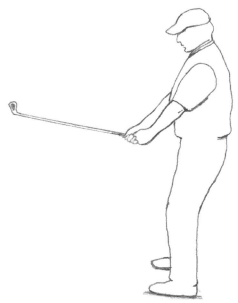

1. Using a 7-iron to start, take your normal stance and address the ball in its normal position.
2. Cock the club in front of you until it is parallel to the ground.
3. Using your shoulders, rotate the club back until you have turned your shoulders 90 degrees (make sure that you do not move your hands).
4. Lift the club normally to the top of your backswing.
5. Fire your hips and shoulders and swing through to the finish. (Your club head should come from the inside, contacting the ball squarely on the ball-target line.)

4

The Number One Fault in Golf

"When it is obvious that the goals cannot be reached, don't adjust the goals, adjust the action steps."

—Confucius

The country western tune, "Looking for love in all the wrong places..." drifts out of the loudspeaker and out across the driving range as the golfers hit balls. Just like the ones they hit before, most of them cut across the patches of grass and dirt from left to right in big sweeping curves, robbing the golfers of both distance and accuracy. How many cumulative yards would it be by now if they could get them all back? How many more will be wasted before they stop swinging out-to-in?

Golfers with this swing problem are found at every range and on every golf course. A conservative estimate would be that nine out of ten golfers swing from out to in. So if the problem is so prevalent, why hasn't someone come up with a cure?

That's where the song comes in. We look for the cure in the wrong places. You can't cure something if you don't understand what's causing it in the first place, and just knowing that the club is coming from outside the ball-target line is not enough to cure the problem. It has long been the standard diagnosis that an out-to-in swing had its roots in a swing that came *over the top*.

Hardly anyone thought it could be wrong if they gave that answer in response to the question, "All my shots are starting left and curving back to the right. What am I doing?" Good friends, lots of instructors would answer with good intentions, "You are swinging over the top, or casting." This is starting the swing with your hands. Some had no idea if that was really your problem, and some did, but it was a well-intended answer and meant to get you to swing inside. Was "swinging over the top" the cause or the symptom of another problem? If you start your swing with your hands you will uncock your wrists too soon, and the club head will end up on a path that is outside the ball target line. If you don't rotate, you will swing on an out-to-in swing path.

Most of the fixes were well intended as well, but since the real problem of the out-to-in path had not been identified, the results were less than satisfactory. Many golfers became frustrated and gave up saying, "It's just the way I swing, and I've learned to live with it. I've tried to fix it, no one can help so I've quit trying and that's that." You don't have to give up; you just have to understand the golf swing and understand why you swing from out to in.

There is not just one issue that results in an out-to-in swing path. There are several potential problems that could be the cause of your slice, or you could have a combination of more than one. You will need to identify what you are doing and choose the proper fundamental or fundamentals to work on to correct your platform or swing. If nine out of ten golfers hit the ball with a slice, then there is something basic that nine out of ten golfers don't understand about swinging a golf club, and that is improper weight management.

Weight management and its effect on club-swing path is the least understood fundamental in golf. Ideally we want to strike the golf ball on a swing path that travels along the ball-target line because this gives the most margin for error, creates the least amount of side spin, and carries the most speed through the ball. In other words we want to strike the ball at the apex of the golf club's swing arc. This would be a swing path from inside the ball-target line into the hitting zone and back inside the ball-target line. This line is sometimes referred to as in-to-out and at other times as in-to-out-to-in.

If we don't accomplish this, the club head travels across the ball-target line from outside to inside and puts sidespin on the ball. The ball may take off straight or slightly to the left or way to the left of our intended target, and then turn back to the right (for right handed golfers). About 90 percent of all golfers play golf with this ball flight. It's called a slice.

In our golf facility we have state of the art golf simulators, and we did considerable testing on golfers of all abilities. We are able to precisely measure club head direction compared to ball-target line. We determined that if the weight is not transferred to the front foot before the swing is started the apex of the swing arc will be at its furthest point just opposite the center or slightly forward of center of the golfer's body. The golfer's effort to transfer his weight to the front foot while swinging does have some effect on the apex, but it does not have sufficient effect to bring the club head inside the ball-target line. Several golfers ended up in a finish that appeared to have transferred the weight to the front foot, but the transfer was late, the swing path was out-to-in and resulted in a slice. When the transfer was late, the golfer hit a slice. It looked like we had a cause-and-effect.

The golf swing is two arms blended into a one-arm swing. That one arm ideally would rotate and swing around a post. We are not equipped to make this movement happen easily, but we can coordinate our bodies to imitate these functions. First let's see what we have to make happen. To assure the front side (post) is fixed and is the point around and from which the swing will rotate and pivot, the weight must be transferred to the left side prior to the beginning of the golf swing. The front shoulder becomes the ball joint from which the arm pivots, and the front hip becomes the axis on which the post rotates.

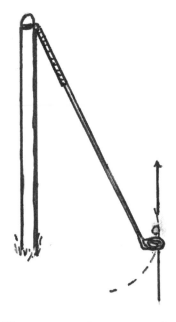

Let's build a perfect swing machine and see what we can learn. It would be fairly simple, if you or I were a post and we had just one arm and one club to rotate around the post. We would just place the ball at the apex of the arc and hit it from the inside every time. So if you think of a post with a pendulum hanging from it you have an idea of what I am thinking of. But although we are not built like that, to achieve the correct results we have to swing like that.

We have two legs and two arms. How do we create a situation where we will be most like the post and the pendulum? If we put equal amounts of weight on both feet and hold the club with both arms straightened and active, and we maintain the same tension in both hands, then the apex of the swing arc ought to be somewhere in the middle of our body. Obviously that solution just won't work. Only one arm can be the pendulum and the other arm will have to act as a stabilizer. Our legs and body will have to become the pole. Makes sense, doesn't it? Next we have to figure out how to stand like a pole. That would mean we have to stand on one leg. We can't do that and maintain our balance, so we have to develop a method that allows us to use our body to imitate a pole that we can rotate around.

We set up in the normal golf stance to achieve balance, and we transfer our weight to our back foot as we wind up (rotate) and then to our front foot as we unwind (rotate) to hit the ball. But, we find out that this doesn't work. We did not establish the front side as post before we rotated. The transfer of weight back to the front involves movement. When the gofer makes the rearward rotation in preparation to swing he is storing energy. Before this energy is released the golfer must establish one fixed post to rotate around. The rotational movement of the legs, hips, torso, and shoulders are the driving forces of the golf swing and these forces must be controlled by one post from the start of the swing. That post is the front side. If you have not shifted your weight to your front side **prior** to beginning your swing, the rotational movement is held back by two posts, and will move the apex of your club arc back in your stance. You will never swing from the inside with accuracy and consistency.

As I said before, the golf swing is really two arms blended into a one-arm swing. The left arm swings (through contact, then both arms are straight together briefly, and then the right takes over to finish the swing) while the remainder of the body and the other arm provides stability and rotation. To assure that the left side (post) is fixed and is the point around which the swing will rotate, the weight must be transferred to the left side prior to the beginning of the golf swing. The front shoulder becomes the ball joint from which the arm swings, and the front hip becomes the axis on which the post (side) rotates. Since I have access to two physicists in my family I took my thoughts to them. After some consideration they returned with this finding: the apex of the arc will follow the center of mass across the golfer's body. This meant that the center of mass would have to be opposite the ball when the ball was struck, or the swing arc will be approaching from an out-to-in path. You can see in Diagrams A, B, and C below that center point of the swing arc is in a different location as a result of the location of the center of mass (COM).

BALL LOCATION

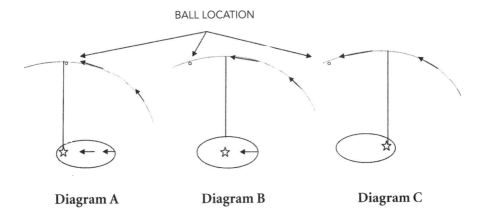

Diagram A   Diagram B   Diagram C

In each diagram above the star represents the golfer's center of mass, COM. The oblong circles represent the golfer's torso. You can see that the arc of the swing path remains the same, but the apex of the swing arc remains opposite the center of mass. As the golfer shifts weight to the front foot, shown by the arrows, the COM moves to the front side (in this case the left side) and the apex of the arc follows. The COM controls the apex of the radius of the swing arc. The apex of the arc controls the out-to-in swing path. In Diagram A the weight has been completely transferred to the left foot (as shown by the two arrows) at the beginning of the swing, and the COM is on the left side of the torso. The swing path will be from in-to-out. In Diagram B the weight is evenly distributed on both feet at impact. The weight shift was late or incomplete, as shown by the one arrow, and the COM ended in the center of the body, resulting in an apex opposite the center of the body and a swing path from out-to-in. In Diagram C the weight has remained on the back foot through impact, no weight shift; the COM is on the back side of the torso and the swing path will be from out-to-in.

Laura's Law was formulated for a pendulum arc of 66 inches (length of the driver and left arm combined) and a center point located at the left shoulder. We considered the left side of the golfer as the pole. The center point of the arc begins in the middle of the golfer, just opposite the chin, when the weight is evenly distributed, and will move toward the rear shoulder (away from the pole) when the golfer shifts his weight to the back foot. A formula was developed to determine how far outside the ball-target line the club head would theoretically go if the weight was not shifted to the front foot prior to beginning the golf swing. In Figures 1 and 2, page 101, you can see that the golfer has transferred his weight prior to beginning the swing, which allows him to rotate around the post on his front side. His COM is aligned with the post and his swing arc will allow him to approach the ball from the in-to-out path.

Now for example, if the center point remains at the chin and is not shifted to the front shoulder by transferring the weight, it will create a 5.4 degree out-to-in swing at the contact point. In Figures 3 and 4, page 102,

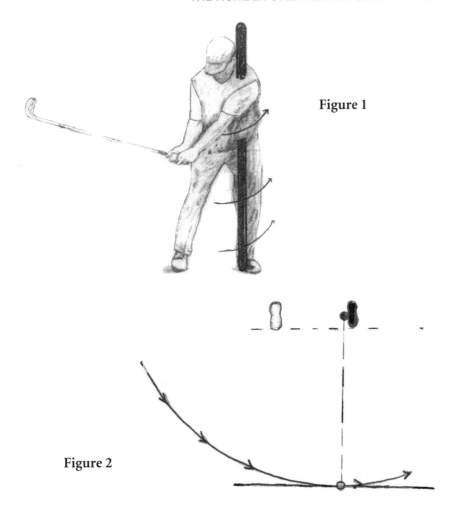

Figure 1

Figure 2

you can see that the golfer has not transferred his weight to his front side prior to beginning his swing. The COM effectively moves the post back across his body and the apex of the swing arc will be outside of the ball target line or on an out-to-in path.

Laura's Law: *Eighty percent of the weight must be transferred to the lead foot prior to beginning the golf swing to effectively establish the post- pendulum relationship necessary to avoid the out-to-in swing path. Degrees off center = arc tan(x in/66 in)*57 deg/rad, where the pendulum arc = arm and club, and x = length in inches between the person's belly button and front leg.*

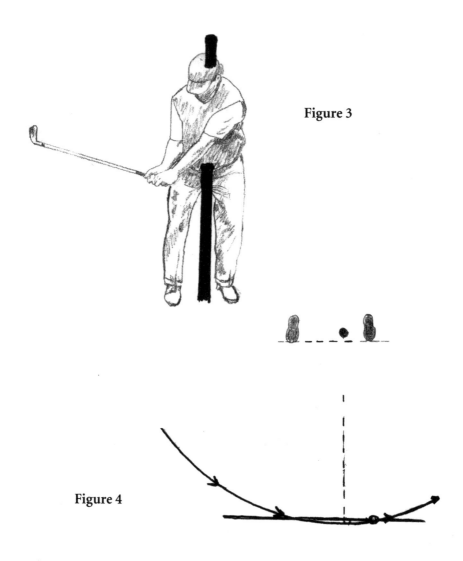

Figure 3

Figure 4

With this explanation, many of you probably now understand the source of your frustration. Golf is a speed game and not a power game. When you think of swinging a golf club, think of throwing a baseball. When you release a baseball the weight is on the front foot. It's the same for golf. Move your weight to the front foot before you swing and you will soon see positive results. Now lets talk about potential problems.

Problems that Cause the Slice

The Push-Off: The first problem you might have is that of too much hitting and not enough swinging. This is someone who learns to play later in life. Usually this person has played other sports and believes that golf is a power sport. The long drive is often the major strength of his game. Hitters are *focused* on the ball.

Hitters push off with the back foot, timing the strike of the ball to coincide with the transfer of the weight to the front foot. There is no weight transfer to the front foot prior to the swing (breaking Laura's Law). This moves the center point of the first pendulum from the front shoulder back across the chest. The swing arc moves outside.

Hitters can also be very handsy (meaning they manipulate the club with their hands instead of just holding it), and lack proper rotation of the hips, torso, and shoulders. This causes swinging from the top with the hands and sends the club on an outside path from the beginning with early uncocking of the wrists. If you fall into this category you have two problems to work on. You will need to quiet your hands and get rid of your push-off.

Low handicappers can also be guilty of the push-off. It is one of the problems that develops when we want to get more power. The tendency to push off is natural. Just understand that staying on the back foot while pushing off is keeping your weight from being on the front foot where you belong. Pushing off is a technique that is employed by most amateurs to obtain additional distance. You must realize that the push-off is a lateral move covering at the most only six inches. This cannot add much speed to the swing of your golf club. By pushing off you are delaying the transfer of weight to the front side, which is a rotary move, moving in the same direction as your shoulders and the head of your golf club. The push-off is timed to transfer the weight from the right foot to the left foot just as the ball is hit. This move keeps the weight from moving to the front foot, causing the swing to come from out-to-in. Your goal should be moving rotationally and ROTATING around your front hip. In order to do so the weight must be on the front foot. Once you start making the change you will find yourself hitting from the inside with the shorter clubs within the first month, but adjusting your swing and the weight shift to the longer clubs will take as much as six months or more. Concentrate on Platform Sections Two, Three, and Four.

You are probably tired of looking for those long balls in the rough anyway.

Lazy Weight Shift: In a lazy weight shift the golfer transfers his weight to his front foot but neglects to do it before he swings. His weight moves to the front foot as he swings. This player has problems with long irons, his driver and fairway woods.

For you to improve you must make your weight shift before your downswing starts. As your club reaches the top of the backswing, release the down pressure on the right foot and rotate the hips. The front hip is the pivot point for the golf swing and the front shoulder becomes the center point of the first swing pendulum. If the front shoulder is not the center point of the swing radius when the swing starts, the swing arc will move out-to-in 0.9 degrees for every inch that the center point moves back across the golfer's chest (Laura's Law).

Alignment: In Section Six of The Platform we discussed how to line up to the ball-target line. Improper alignment can produce an out-to-in swing problem. Aiming your body either left or right of the ball-target line while you focus on the ball will produce an out-to-in swing path. This is caused by your hands and arms trying to correct for your improper alignment. Stance and alignment are closely related, and mistakes in either one make a repeatable in-to-out-to-in swing impossible. Reread both sections, Stance and Alignment, and make sure you understand the fundamentals of both. If alignment is your only problem you should be swinging in-to-out-to-in in a very short time.

Big Backswing: If your backswing passes parallel at the top it can be the problem or part of the problem. Big backswings do not automatically contribute to faster swing speeds. Most often they only contribute to higher scores. The big backswing causes you to become handsy at the top and loosen your grip on the club. When the hands get involved you can create all kinds of errors in your shots. It is one cause of casting the club outside from the top of the swing. Shorting the backswing is the cure. Practice the cocking drill. Keep the hands firm at the top. This can be accomplished with about one month's hard work. Concentrate on Chapter Three.

Straight Right Leg: During the backswing there is a tendency to straighten the right leg. When the back leg straightens, the back shoulder is in a higher position than it was at address. As the swing begins the first pendulum (arm pendulum) no longer drops down and inside. If you straighten your leg on the takeaway it may be causing you to swing out-to-in. Work on keeping your right knee bent and the weight to the inside of your right foot throughout the backswing. Go back to Section Three. This is a problem that you can work on away from the golf course, and in about sixty days you should have it corrected.

No Separation: When you rotate you must have separation between the hip and shoulder rotation. This separation is 45 degrees. If there is no separation or insufficient separation between the hip rotation and the shoulder rotation, this will cause the shoulders to over-rotate and align themselves open to the ball-target line. This will cause the first pendulum to swing on an out-to-in swing path. This problem is usually combined with footwork problems. Check your right foot. Is it perpendicular to the ball-target line? You can expect to take about three months or more to correct these problems. Concentrate on Sections Two, Three, and Four.

Second Pendulum: The release of the second pendulum (the wrist cock) in relation to the alignment of your shoulders is critical to the in-to-out-to-in swing path. The fundamentals are fairly basic and deal with the laws of physics. Remember, the second pendulum will be traveling in an opposite direction from the first pendulum if you do not make a full shoulder turn on your backswing. In order for the second pendulum to match up with first pendulum and swing along the ball-target line, it must be released while the shoulders are turned to the rear (closed) to the ball-target line. That is where the two pendulums line up. You do not control this release, but you need to make a sufficient shoulder turn so that it can happen. If you try to control this timing you will either release too early and end up casting from the top, which produces an out-to-in swing path, or release too late, which produces an out-to-in path. In either case trying to control the release is not a solution. The solution is to let it happen.

You can get a good feel for what happens by setting up facing a wall. To start use a short iron. Make your normal backswing and wrist cock. Watch as you slowly return the club to the ball. The uncocking of the club must occur while the shoulders are turned to the rear or there will not be enough room for you to swing through without hitting the wall. Swing the club with increasing speed until you are comfortable that you will not hit the wall. Expect to take about thirty days to correct this problem. Concentrate on Section Four and Chapter Three.

5

Author's Notes

To round out this book I have put together a few thoughts on the game that have accumulated over the years. Some of them make for fun reading and others merit some serious thought. But in all they just represent topics that you and I might discuss on a warm afternoon following a lesson or round of golf while we sit at the nineteenth hole stretching the truth just a little.

I hope you have enjoyed reading this book and it provides you with some new insights into the game of golf. Teaching golf is what I love to do and getting to write about it has been an extraordinary opportunity. Perhaps someday we will meet for a mutually rewarding learning session or a round of golf . . .

Hogan's Secret

Ben Hogan's book, *Five Lessons, The Modern Fundamentals of Golf* is one of the best-selling golf books in history. In the foreword written by *Sports Illustrated's* managing editor Sidney James the reader is promised revelations of the swing by the man who has learned "the secret of good, of great golf." The revelations were first published in *Sports Illustrated* and later in the book form. What Hogan's secret was all about is still a mystery to most who have read and reread Hogan's book. Mr. Hogan is very clear about what he writes in his book and the special move he makes with his wrists. He explains the move that allows him to swing as hard as he wants from the inside and still hit a fade. It is carefully described and supported by drawings in his book. Or is it?

Without question Ben Hogan had a *secret*. Even for the most talented ball striker what he did would seem impossible, but Hogan backed it up. His drives reached 300 yards with persimmon woods, and he hit green after green, and this was in the 1950s. It is obvious that Mr. Hogan had something to teach all of us about striking a golf ball. Countless teachers have tried to explain what the book says that allowed Hogan to deliver so much club-head speed to the ball. Each had a slightly different take on Hogan's secret.

The fact is Mr. Hogan's secret has really never been a secret. But the secret is not in his book. Mr. Hogan revealed the fix for his secret in the August 8, 1955 issue of *Life* magazine. He then discusses the fix again when he wrote his book in 1957, but the fix does not tell us the real reason why he could hit the ball so far. He doesn't tell us because he felt the secret was too hard for amateurs to handle. So what was Ben Hogan leaving out?

Let's discuss what we do know. It's hard to imagine that what Dr. David Hallberg told us over forty years ago at Macalester College in an anatomy and kinesiology class would prove valuable in a discussion about Ben Hogan's golf swing, but here we go. The move, the one that made Hogan's career, had everything to do with supination and pronation. But, not the supination and pronation that Mr. Hogan writes about in his book.

Supination is rotation of the forearm to turn the wrist so that the palm of the hand will face skyward. Pronation is rotation of the forearm to turn the wrist so the palm of the hand would face toward the ground. The key action is the *rotation of the forearm*. We have to rotate the forearm to supinate and to pronate. The actions do not occur if we don't rotate the forearm. The terms come from the muscles controlling the actions and they are located in the forearms, the supinators and

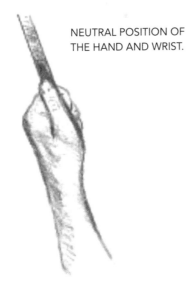

NEUTRAL POSITION OF
THE HAND AND WRIST.

ROTATION OF THE FOREARM
COUNTERCLOCKWISE PRODUCES
SUPINATION.

pronators. Ben Hogan did not write about supination and pronation in his book. I know he uses the words supination and pronation, but he uses them incorrectly.

So what did Ben Hogan write about? In his book he is very careful to avoid any discussion about an action involving the rolling of his arms or hands. Mr. Hogan states, "The player who thinks he can construct a swing on hand action and who, since this is impossible, is doomed to be erratic." Instead he discusses *cupping* of his wrists which he errantly calls supination and pronation, claiming this move alone allowed him to achieve the tremendous increase in power. Mr. Hogan also states that there is no danger that the "right hand will overpower the left and twist the club over. It can't. As far as applying power goes I wish I had three right hands." That is one of the most confusing statements ever written in a golf instruction book. There is no twisting movement involved in cupping of the wrists. Search and search in his book, but you can't find out what he does with his right hand to make him wish he had three of them.

Mr. Hogan demonstrates what he says is his secret move, first by the throwing of a baseball half side arm and half underhand. Throwing the ball as shown with the right elbow close to the hip does not require the hand or wrist to twist, pronate or supinate, but the right wrist does cup.

ROTATION OF
THE FOREARM
CLOCKWISE
PRODUCES
PRONATION.

This cupping move is called flexion and extension. Mr. Hogan demonstrates the secret move for us in this manner without the golf club so that we might see exactly what the right wrist does in the swing. You can see by the release of the ball that it is the wrist that moves, while the right hand remains in the neutral position. Because it does not rotate, it neither pronates nor supinates.

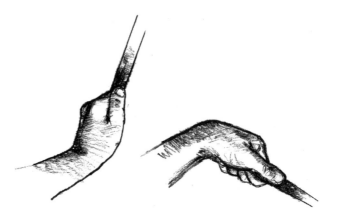

BENDING THE WRIST IN TOWARD
THE BODY IS FLEXION.

EXTENDING THE WRIST OUT AWAY
FROM THE BODY IS EXTENSION.

Next he demonstrates the two-handed basketball pass. We see the same action, but in this case we see both hands involved much the same as they would be in a golf swing. The difference being they are not holding a club, but passing a medicine ball. We see the right wrist *extend* and *flex* while the left wrist *flexes* and then *extends*. The hands remain in the neutral position; there is no supination or pronation of either hand.

He then matches these two examples with an example of his swing to demonstrate that what he his telling us actually happens in the golf swing. *There is no supination or pronation in the golf swing that he demonstrates.*

The hands are in the neutral position and do not move throughout the swing, but we do see the left wrist *flexing* as the swing moves toward contact with the ball.

When Mr. Hogan describes his secret he does it in this manner: "In the sequence, there is one position of such signal importance that it warrants close-up study. This is the position of the left wrist and hand at the actual moment of impact. AT IMPACT THE BACK OF THE LEFT HAND FACING TOWARD THE TARGET IS ACTUALLY RAISED. IT POINTS TO THE TARGET AND, AT THE MOMENT THE BALL IS CONTACTED, IT IS OUT IN FRONT, NEARER TO THE TARGET THAN ANY OTHER PART OF THE HAND."

When Mr. Hogan describes his "secret" move in his book he only includes the flexion of the left wrist. When this is done *extension* of the right wrist must occur to accommodate the movement. This is only part of his secret move. *Flexion* of the left wrist and *extension* of the right wrist delofts the club, allowing for a crisper strike of the ball and a lower ball flight. Hardly the thing that makes 300-yard drives.

Now we come to the second part of the secret. How did Ben Hogan manage to leave the face of the club open? He wanted to swing hard with both hands, but never have his right hand dominate the golf swing (But remember he wanted three right hands). So he changed his grip. He didn't just weaken his grip. He strengthened his left hand on the club by moving it on top, and then he neutralized his right hand by moving it on top as well with the right-hand thumb forefinger V located past his left hand thumb forefinger V so that it pointed at his chin, while the V of the left hand grip pointed at his right eye.

The stated purpose of Mr. Hogan's grip change was to allow him to swing as hard as he wanted without closing the face of the club at impact. This would allow him to always hit a slight fade. Why such a drastic change in the grip if there was not something else going on in Mr. Hogan's golf swing? In the drawings we see in his book there in nothing to indicate that such a drastically weak grip is a requirement.

We have Mr. Hogan with *flexion* (remember he called it supination) of the left wrist just prior to contact and a super weak grip swinging as hard as he wants without ever hitting a draw. This in itself does not give us the recipe for 300 yard drives with persimmon woods in 1950. There had to be something else. Confusion followed as analyst after analyst tried to explain what Mr. Hogan really meant to say.

What has Mr. Hogan told us? Actually, he told us nothing at all about his real secret in his book. If you didn't read the 1985 story in *Golf Digest* where, Hogan said, "The idea is to rotate the club with my left arm," you would have never known his real *secret*. Ben Hogan did supinate and pronate. Only he called it *rolling* his arms. He did it successfully and it was the primary reason that a man of his slight build could hit a ball such a great distance. The rolling of his forearms gave added speed to his swing. Of course with the discrepancy in the use of terms causing considerable confusion it's unlikely the average golfer would ever understand Hogan's secret. As a caddy Mr. Hogan learned that rolling his hands provided a low trajectory draw that sometimes turned into a hook. The low rolling ball was perfectly suited for Texas terrain.

Rolling the forearms opened the clubface on the backswing and rolling the clubface closed on the downswing added speed, but was erratic and was the cause of Mr. Hogan's terrible hook. He cured his hook with his

HOGAN'S
WEAK GRIP.

uniquely weak grip and his cupped (flexed) left wrist, which he incorrectly identified as supinated.

Earlier in this book I wrote that there "is no supination or pronation" in the golf swing and I will stick to that statement, except when it comes to Ben Hogan. I will warn those who seek to emulate him that you will have to adopt some unorthodox methods to master the use of the *forearm roll* (supination and pronation). Mr. Hogan's grip was about as unorthodox as they come. He employed not just a weak grip, but a grip that moved the right hand so far on top of the club that it was completely negated by the position of the left hand. This prevented the right hand from ever dominating the swing as it pronated on the downswing. In addition Mr. Hogan employed the flexion movement of the left wrist and the corresponding extension of the right wrist, which in effect blocked the pronation and delofted the club. I would guess those two changes and about five or six hours of practice a day would be sufficient. Come to think of it, that's what Mr. Hogan did.

Ben Hogan did not think that his real secret was for the masses (I agree), and for that reason he excluded it from his book. His one error was that he mistakenly used the terms supination and pronation, instead of flexion and extension, in describing a part of his secret, and by doing so the two words have lived on in the golf lexicon for the past fifty-plus years describing something they are not. They have confused all who knew their meaning, and misinformed all who did not.

Only someone as revered as Mr. Hogan could have made this happen.

Practice

There is an old Chinese proverb that says "Learning is like rowing upstream, not to advance is to drop back." This is as apt a description of the game of golf as you will ever find. You must practice to improve and to maintain whatever level of proficiency you have achieved. If you do not practice, your skills will slowly erode.

I spent a lot of time in the manufacturing industry and one of the many sets of buzz words that came along during my tenure was the concept of zero defects, in other words, perfection. It sounded great, but just how is something like that to be achieved? We were working with machines capable of producing parts to tolerances measured in ten thousandths of an inch, measured by lasers, with repeatability that wasn't interrupted by sore or tiring muscles, controlled by unflinching computers not brain cells subject to thoughts of disaster around the corner, and yet we couldn't reach our goals of zero defects.

So what do we do with the human body? Errors are going to occur and we are going to have to deal with those errors. Our brains get filled with thoughts of disaster and we have to deal with them while our opponents are enjoying success. In business we spent our money and time in the areas where it would bring the most return. To me that also makes sense for the game of golf.

Practice the shots that will do you the most good. Take what limited time you have to practice and divide it among the clubs you play the most often on the golf course. If you play almost all your rounds at your home course then you know what clubs those will be. If you have time to round out your game, then practice with other clubs. Most golfers will focus on the driver, wedge, and putter. Don't just practice with the club you hit the best. To score you need to learn to get up and down around the green. The quickest way for most golfers to improve their scores is to devote about 60 to 70 percent of available time to the short game, and about 30 to 40 percent of the time to hitting the driver and iron shots.

Random Practice: If you are learning a new motor skill, studies have now shown that random practice is the best stimulator for the brain. Random practice is practice that constantly changes the practice situation; this requires the brain to reset itself each time the skill is used. You just don't hit the same shot over and over. So how do your get your groove? Well, you don't. What you do is learn in a situation similar to playing. You don't get do-overs on the course, and this learning method puts your brain through the entire process each time you hit a ball. Studies say that this resetting the brain process has more positive results in learning retention over the long term.

So if you are learning something new, use variety in practice. Change the distance and clubs frequently and don't make practice routine. Challenge yourself to create excitement during your practice by setting goals, making every practice a contest, and keeping score.

Block Practice: If you are working on a learned motor skill, block practice can be the best, but you will need to keep your mind challenged. Block practice is hitting the same shot repeatedly. Hitting balls over and over will not make your neuron bundle stronger unless there is some reason that creates excitement in the synapse. Just as the brain is able to block out the sound of a highway or a train that passes by your house at night, it will also block out the repetitive action of your golf swing unless it is accompanied by some stimulus. You might as well be playing catch or lifting dumbbells. So if you are going to use the block practice method make sure that you get your brain actively involved by making each shot important. You can do this by going through your routine and putting emphasis on making each shot perfect. Get a partner and wager or have contests in order to make each shot important. Don't just hit shot after shot.

Visualization

I know it seems a lot like daydreaming, but it really works. And before you start thinking I've stepped on the third rail crossing the tracks trying to catch the crosstown bullet, let me tell you that we don't have anything more dangerous than a bus here in Steamboat. So when I say visualization I'm not inviting you to think I'm a weirdo. I'm just a guy who would investigate, try, and recommend anything I find that works. Visualization works. Like any new skill the more you do it the better you are at it, and the better you are the better it works. If you are sloppy and expect immediate results you are going to get sloppy results.

The best times to do this are just before you go to sleep and just after you wake up. The optimum amount of time is about five to ten minutes. To succeed in visualization, keep the input positive, stay focused during the session, and keep the session short. Multiple short sessions are more effective than one longer session. Limit the motor skill variables during any one session.

I have read enough and had enough feedback from others to know, that positive results are there for the taking. I have experienced success myself. It helps me with my golf game and it can help you with yours.

Here is what you do. You work on one part of your game at a time. If it is putting then you start with lining up the putt, reading the break, picking your line, everything you would do before you address the ball. Then visualize yourself setting up to the ball and try to feel the putter in your hands. As you do this make everything as real as it can be. Visualize the club going back and through with a perfect stroke, and watch the ball roll along the line you have picked and into the hole. I work on five-foot putts only. Those are the putts I have to make on the course to improve my scores.

Helpful Reminders

➤ No matter who you are, take time to warm up before you play. This is important for your body and for your mind.
  ▪ Stretching
  ▪ Hitting balls
  ▪ Walking around the parking lot
  ▪ Situps, pushups, and other stretching followed by a shower—this is nice
➤ Your first shot on the course is the most important of the day. Relax and take a club that will allow you to hit the ball in the fairway.
➤ There are no unimportant shots in a round of golf. If you begin to feel like your next shot is unimportant, stop and rearrange your thinking.
➤ Keep the grip, the alignment, the stance, and the ball position all neutral.
➤ Golf starts *from the ground up* so the first move is the weight shift.
➤ Make a 90 degree shoulder turn and keep your hands in front of you throughout the backswing.
➤ Keep your emotions positive. Be positive on the tee and before every shot. Don't let negative thoughts get in the way. If they do, step back and reload.
➤ Limit emotional reaction to bad shots. It's not only bad form, but it creates a chemical release in your brain that actually increases the chances that you will reproduce that shot again.
➤ Often we feel like we should practice and then practice some more. Well, your brain will get tired long before your body. So break up your practice sessions into 30-minute blocks.

➤ You often hear the advice "hit down on the ball," when playing your iron shots. If you try to follow that advice literally by hitting down on the ball you will end up with a steep swing and trying to delay uncocking your wrists. The advice is meant to encourage you to maintain your swing arc through the ball and let your club take a divot after hitting the ball. The club choice, your stance and ball placement will determine the bottom of your swing arc and the amount and length of your divot.

➤ Learn the feel of your swing. Especially the feel of different distances with your wedges and your putter. Practice with your eyes closed whenever you can.

➤ Big scores come from penalty shots. Plan your strategy to avoid them.

➤ When teeing off learn to hit your driver in the fairway, or pick a club that you can.

➤ If in doubt on any shot, play away from trouble. A bogey beats a double bogey anytime.

➤ Getting up and down around the green will save you a bundle of strokes, plus it increases your confidence on your second shot because the greens seem to get bigger when you are confident about getting up and down.

➤ Become a master of the five-foot putt.

➤ Break up your practice time this way: 30 percent putter, 30 percent short game, and 40 percent irons and driver.

➤ If you are thinking about hitting an old ball to avoid putting a good ball in a hazard, then it's probably the wrong club, or the wrong shot.

Ball Flight Rules

The laws of physics are in charge of the golf ball. The dimples on the ball are there to produce lift. Without the dimples, the golf ball would only fly about half as far. Every golf ball manufacturer has its engineers working overtime to discover which combination of dimples or pattern will achieve the optimal flight.

The same physics laws are in charge of where the ball will go when it is struck by the golf club. The first rule is direction. The golf ball will travel in the direction that the club is traveling when it hits the ball, except for a glancing blow. When you see the initial direction of your ball flight you can determine your swing path. It is a cause and effect situation. If you swing straight through the hitting zone, the ball will go straight. If you swing through the hitting zone from out-to-in (right to left) the ball will go left. If you swing through the hitting zone from in-to-out (left to right) the ball will go right. (Opposite description for left handers).

The laws of physics also control the clubface. If the clubface is square it will not impart spin on the golf ball, and the ball will continue in the

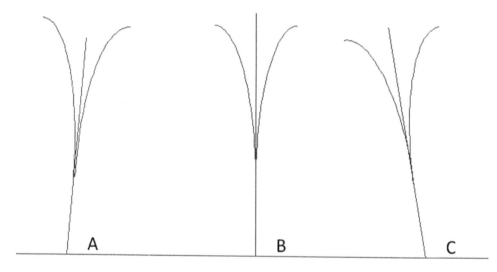

IN THE RULES OF BALL FLIGHT THE DIRECTION IS INITIALLY CONTROLLED BY THE DIRECTION OF THE CLUBHEAD. AS YOU CAN SEE ABOVE THE CLUB IN EACH CASE (A, B, C) WAS TRAVELING IN A DIFFERENT DIRECTION WHEN IT CONTACTED THE BALL. THE CLUBHEAD IN THE EXAMPLE B WOULD HAVE BEEN THE ONE TRAVELING DOWN THE BALL-TARGET LINE. IN THE CASES WHERE THE BALL TURNS TO THE LEFT THE CLUBFACE WAS **CLOSED** AT IMPACT AND CREATED COUNTER-CLOCKWISE SPIN, WHICH EVENTUALLY CAUSED THE BALL TO TURN TO THE LEFT. IN THE CASES WHERE THE BALL TURNED TO THE RIGHT THE CLUBFACE WAS **OPEN** AT IMPACT, CREATING A CLOCKWISE SPIN CAUSING THE BALL TO TURN TO THE RIGHT. IF YOU PAY ATTENTION TO YOUR BALL FLIGHT, YOU WILL LEARN A LOT ABOUT YOUR BALL STRIKING.

swing direction. If the clubface is open, the club will impart a clockwise spin on the ball. It will fly along the direction it was hit to begin with, and the spin will cause it to turn to the right. If the clubface is closed, the ball will fly along the direction it was hit to begin with, and then the spin will cause it to turn to the left.

Each of the diagrams shows a swing path and a clubface angle and the corresponding ball flight. Study them and you will be able to understand why you produced certain shot shapes.

Creep

Creep is one of the eternal enemies of all mankind, and not just in golf—he is everywhere day and night. His attacks are relentless. Our only defense is to acknowledge that he exists and to develop methods to combat him when and where we can. Not every battle is worth fighting; I learned that lesson from my wife. But the battle against creep on the golf course is one we cannot ignore and we cannot afford to lose. So, let's talk about what we can do to win.

Creep is the slow erosion in the quality of what we do. Just little things that are slightly different, not quite enough to notice, but over time the deterioration accumulates and eventually it makes a difference. It's that old "stitch in time" routine. Colors creep, measurements creep, the wear on your grips creeps, your grip itself creeps, your stance and alignment can creep. We would never simply pace off the dimensions to our new home or guess at the weight of the steak we are buying at the butcher, no matter how familiar we were with the length of our gait or the feel of a pound of meat. But we casually grip our clubs, guess at distances to the pin, and align ourselves while we are playing golf. My question is, How often do we check our grip, the real distance to the pin, or measure our gait or recheck our alignment?

Are you making absolutely certain that you have given yourself a 100 percent chance to hit the very best shot possible? People who take measurements for a living have their equipment checked out regularly, because they are aware that it is subject to creep–those slight variations that can throw off the results and cost them money, perhaps even make a building fall down—and they want to be accurate. Do you think that your personal equipment, your eyes (your rangefinder), your stance (tripod), your hands (gear holder), have gone through the season without any changes and will set up the same way every time?

Maybe you are aiming to the right, or you are too close, or too far from the ball. What if you have changed your grip just so slightly everyday and you haven't realized it? Creep is a deadly adversary if you don't keep him in check. Have your local pro, or your golfing buddy give your platform a complete check-out once a month. What about your equipment? Worn grips are a major source of bad shots. If you are a frequent player check your grips for wear regularly and, at least once a year, have your pro shop check the loft and lie on your irons.

Don't let creep turn a par into a bogey.

Origin of the Term Par

I have often wondered if golf would be as much fun to play if it wasn't so hard. When you think about it even the very best golfers in the world don't shoot *par* all the time, and there are times on certain holes when they just blow it all up. It happens more frequently on the local level with local pros and low handicappers. I suspect we have all rejoiced to see that humility rides in everybody's golf bag.

There was a time however when bogey was the score everyone attempted to achieve. It was the acceptable score. Par didn't exist! Wow! Think what your course would play like if bogey was the acceptable score? When par didn't exist some adjustments were made to the bogey score, so to compare accurately you could only adjust par at your course about 14 strokes. That would make par about 86. Would you really be happier? I think not.

I don't think we really want our game to be easier. I think what we find most discouraging about accepting par is not the difficulty of the score, but more the word par itself. In the dictionary par is defined as equal, common status, the average or normal state. That description places nearly everyone who plays the game as being unable to attain the level of normal or average play. Now, that's discouraging. If the definition of par were something like terrific or outstanding, or perfect and we couldn't quite make the grade, it would be more understandable, but to call the goal par (in effect making it average) really, it seems somewhat cruel.

If I tell you how it got the name par you are going to see the irony in it all. The first golf rating system for handicaps was developed by the Ladies Golf Union in Great Britain. They had the choice of two systems and chose the one that designated the proper score for each hole to be called par, and dropped the higher score of bogey. When the system was brought to the U.S. the Massachusetts Men's Golf Association wanted to preserve the easier bogey, but the USG adopted par as the standard for the handicap system. So it is as it should be. Ladies who are golf widows all around the world may rejoice in the knowledge that men who will forever sneak off leaving lawns unmowed, houses unpainted, and garages cluttered with junk are doing so in an attempt to score only average at the game of golf. And this is all due to the foresight of one English lady named Issette Pearson. Sadly, average is a level that very few of them will ever achieve.

Watch Out for Stupid

I suspect that everyone will admit to doing something stupid every now and then, and most of us will admit that we didn't need any help getting it done. The problem in the game of golf is when it comes to doing stupid things you get help, and I feel that it's my obligation to warn you about where that help comes from. Let's imagine you find yourself on the tee box with 155 yards of carry over water, and you know your best shot ever with a six-iron carried 165 yards. You choose a six-iron. You do this partially because your buddies are hitting six irons, and partially out of the belief you can hit it that far. Well, you no longer have to blame yourself, or that sudden unseen burst of wind that must have caught your ball, or any other imagined problem that caused your ball to fall short. Just blame Stupid.

Because anywhere the game of golf is played, Stupid is lurking. While you were considering the five iron that you should have hit, Stupid reminded you that you once hit a six iron 165 yards, and he also asked you if you wanted to look like a sissy in front of your friends? Stupid is like that. He will brag on you, and he will shame you in the same breath, and the single purpose is to get you to hit the wrong shot.

So, how am I so sure that Stupid exists? The answer is easy. I've been playing this game for over fifty years, and Stupid has visited me and my golfing buddies on numerous occasions. He has ruined holes, he has ruined rounds. There is good probability that he has ruined lives. I have seen golf clubs in trees, golf bags in lakes, golf carts in ditches, grown men crying, wives wrestling the checkbooks from their husbands' hands. I have seen men knocked out by their own golf ball, and I have seen errant shots go places you wouldn't believe. Stupid visited me enough times during my younger days that I had an exorcism done on my golf bag. Even today I regularly empty its contents looking for evidence that he might have taken up residence once again. Stupid is an evil, evil character. We all remember what he did to our hero Roy McAvoy in the movie *Tin Cup*.

Sadly he just doesn't strike in the movies, or unknown golfers. In 1999 we watched Stupid crawl out of the Barry Burn at Carnoustie and into the golf bag of Jean Van de Velde, who would have been the most improbable winner of the British Open in modern times. He struck more than one time that day showing not only that he is devious, but persistent. In 2006 we all watched as he struck again, and this time it was the most the probable winner of the U.S. Open who fell prey to his guile. Hiding this time in the trees along the patron's tents and despite all the security, he dropped into Phil Mickelson's bag at a time when Mickelson had the championship within his grasp. A safe play out to the fairway and a shot to the green saves the championship for Phil. But, demonstrating that the high and mighty are as vulnerable as the average golfer, Phil let it slip because Stupid whispered sweet nothings into his ear, and he believed. He believed Stupid to the tune of a double bogey.

Here are a few clues that Stupid is talking. My advice: don't listen.

1. You can get between those trees. (When you are having a hard time seeing between them. You will get to hit this shot again; you'll just be under the trees next time.)
2. Just open the face and hit a lob shot. (When you have only hit about three lob shots in your life and none has worked. This is one of Stupid's favorite pieces of advice. Hit a shot you have not practiced or mastered. As far as he's concerned you're brilliant. Take it from me, you're not. Hit something you have confidence in.)
3. You can still save par. (Stupid will say this most often just before you hit the shot that gets you a double or triple bogey. Play for the bogey.)
4. Let's go for a little extra distance. (Stupid says this just before you hit that giant slice into the woods on the right. Back off, reset your platform and go for right down the middle.)
5. You are between clubs. Let's take one less club and hit it hard. (Stupid likes the shots where the turf goes farther than the ball. Take one more, choke down and swing normal.)
6. Sure, it's a narrow fairway, go ahead, hit the driver. (This is real good advice when you haven't hit your driver in the fairway all day. Pick something that will get the ball in play.)
7. You are teeing the ball close to the road and about to start your backswing when a truck roars by with the horn blaring. Be cool, act like it didn't bother you. (No way, back off and start your routine over again.)

Stupid can cost you strokes every round, and they are not strokes lost because of poor play. Make good decisions. Check your bag for Stupid on a regular basis. It's worth the effort.

Index